METHODOLOGIES, MODELS AND INSTRUMENTS FOR RURAL AND URBAN LAND MANAGEMENT

Methodologies, Models and Instruments for Rural and Urban Land Management

Edited by

MARK DEAKIN
Napier University, UK

ROBERT DIXON-GOUGH
University of East London, UK

REINFRIED MANSBERGER
Universität für Bodenkultur, Austria

LONDON AND NEW YORK

First published 2004 by Ashgate Publishing

Published 2016 by Routledge
2 Park Square, Milton Park, Abingdon, Oxon OX14 4RN
711 Third Avenue, New York, NY 10017, USA

Routledge is an imprint of the Taylor & Francis Group, an informa business

Copyright © 2004 Mark Deakin, Robert Dixon-Gough and Reinfried Mansberger

Mark Deakin, Robert Dixon-Gough and Reinfried Mansberger have asserted their right under the Copyright, Designs and Patents Act, 1988, to be identified as the editors of this work.

All rights reserved. No part of this book may be reprinted or reproduced or utilised in any form or by any electronic, mechanical, or other means, now known or hereafter invented, including photocopying and recording, or in any information storage or retrieval system, without permission in writing from the publishers.

Notice:
Product or corporate names may be trademarks or registered trademarks, and are used only for identification and explanation without intent to infringe.

British Library Cataloguing in Publication Data
Methodologies, models and instruments for rural and urban
    land management. - (International land management series)
    1.Land use - Management - Congresses 2.City planning -
    Congresses 3.Rural development - Congresses
    I.Deakin, Mark II.Dixon-Gough, R. W. (Robert W)
    III.Mansberger, Reinfried IV.International Land Management
    Conference (2nd : 1999 : Danbury, England)
    333.7'3

Library of Congress Cataloging-in-Publication Data
Methodologies, models and instruments for rural and urban land management / edited by
    Mark Deakin, Robert Dixon-Gough, Reinfried Mansberger.
       p. cm. -- (International land management series)
    Includes bibliographical references and index.
    ISBN 0-7546-3415-9
    1. Land use, Rural--Planning--Congresses. 2. Land use, Urban--Planning--Congresses.
    3. Land use--Environmental aspects--Congresses. I.Deakin, Mark. II.Dixon-Gough, R.
    W. III. Mansberger, Reinfried. IV. International Land Management Conference (2nd :
    1999 : Danbury, England) V. Series.

    HD1393.M475 2004
    333.73--dc22

2004041044

Transfered to Digital Printing in 2012

ISBN 9780754634157 (hbk)
ISBN 9781138247413 (pbk)

Contents

1	Introduction *Mark Deakin, Robert Dixon-Gough and Reinfried Mansberger*	1
2	Partnership, Process, and Planning in Estuary Management: The Case of the Lower Thames *Robert Home*	5
3	Land Reform in Developing Countries: Legal and Institutional Aspects *Alec McEwen*	16
4	International Land Management: Aspects on Education and Training *Reinfried Mansberger and Erwin Heine*	24
5	Land Fragmentation in Central Europe: How and Whether to use Western Experience *Terry van Dijk*	35
6	The Implementation Framework of Legal Systems *Ninel Jasmine Sadjadi*	49
7	Mediation in Land Consolidation and in Boundary Disputes *Jørn Rognes and Per Kåre Sky*	59
8	Policy Instruments in the Changing Context of Dutch Land Development *Daniëlle Groetelaers and Willem Korthals Altes*	75
9	Modelling the Development of Sustainable Communities in Edinburgh's South East Wedge *Mark Deakin*	88
10	The Redevelopment of the Railway Lands of London's King's Cross: Actors, Agendas, and Processes *Emmanuel Mutale*	104
11	BEQUEST: Sustainable Urban Development, the Framework, and Directory of Assessment Methods *Mark Deakin and Steve Curwell*	121

12	Object Model for Temporal Changes in Geographical Information Systems	
	Abdul Adamu, Souhiel Khaddaj and Munir Morad	137
13	Using GIS Techniques to Evaluate Community Sustainability in Open Forestlands in Sub-Saharan Africa	
	Yang Li, Alan Grainger, Zoltan Hesley, Ole Hofstad,	
	Prem Lal Sankhayan, Ousmane Diallo and Aku O'Kting'Ati	146
14	Community Participation in Rural and Urban Development	
	Robert Dixon-Gough, Reinfried Mansberger and Mark Deakin	164
Index		*170*

Chapter 1

Introduction

Mark Deakin, Robert Dixon-Gough and Reinfried Mansberger

Introduction

Throughout the last decade, environmental issues have become increasingly important in all aspects of rural and urban development. Added to this is the increasing pressure being experienced virtually throughout the world upon urban areas as a result of migration from rural regions. Much of this pressure is in the peri-urban areas, although as the result of an increasingly urbanised population many of the policies that are being formulated at governmental levels are viewed by rural dwellers as having an increasingly urban emphasis.

This book identifies many of the problems relating to rural and urban development at the beginning of the 20th century and considers certain methodologies, models and instruments that may be used to reduce conflicts in the development process. The book is a presentation of edited papers that were presented at the Second International Land Management Conference, which took place at Danbury, Essex in 1999. Certain papers were selected for inclusion within this book and have been updated, extensively reviewed, edited, and revised in the context of land management and land administration.

The first group of papers considers the importance of co-operation and partnerships, institutional aspects, and the importance of education and training. The framework is set by Home in Chapter 2, who outlines the importance of partnerships and planning in the context of the development of the Thames Estuary. The concept of partnerships is very relevant in the case of many geographical entities since they often extend beyond normal administrative boundaries, whether they are local, regional, national, or transnational. Home examines the evolution and types of partnerships that are relevant to rural and urban development although the main thrust of this chapter is upon their relevance to the formulation and implementation of a strategy for a specific purpose.

In the following chapter, McEwen provides an overview of the importance of legal and institutional aspects in the context of land reform. This chapter considers the philosophical questions of land ownership and land use by taking a number of specific examples, ranging from the 'First Nations' of Canada, to the situation in countries as geographically diverse as Zanzibar and Mongolia. McEwen considers that the legal instruments relating to land should reflect both the customary practices and the will of the people, factors that have been neglected by many consultants in transitional countries over the past 15 years. He provides many interesting case studies based upon his very wide experience. The importance of institutions is similarly emphasised since their availability is the key to land reform and land development. McEwen considers that local institutions are essential in maintaining links with the people, a role somewhat similar to that of the partnerships described by Home. The final point made in this chapter is the role and importance of technology, particularly the inter-relationship between the application of modern technology and the availability of trained operators, a factor that should be noted by those involved in training and education throughout the world.

The role of education and training in international land management is the theme of Mansberger and Heine who consider that the responsibility of 'knowledge-transfer' lies in the hands of a multiplicity of organisations, ranging from governments through to the deliverers in the form of educational institutions. The authors emphasise that land management is a complex discipline that requires knowledge from a wide range of fields. In order to fulfil the functions of land management, it is important for those being educated or trained to understand the inter-relationship between technologies and methodologies. However, they also have to be aware of the availability and nature of data needed to model and simulate particular situations. Underpinning this is an awareness and appreciation of the relevance and nature of adequate legal instruments pertaining to models and the development of the rural and urban infrastructures. One of the key recommendations of this chapter is the need for constant and continuing vocational training to keep practitioners abreast of current improvements in technology, data processing, planning methods, and legal instruments.

The next group of chapters concentrates on particular legal instruments relating to land management. In Chapter 5, van Dijk considers the emergence of land fragmentation in Central Europe, together with the degree of severity of the problem. One of the questions posed in this chapter is why fragmentation is perceived to be a problem by land managers. This gives rise to some interesting comparisons concerning the relative merits of small farms and whether they are capable of sustaining full-time farming. Finally, van Dijk presents a comparative evaluation of the legal instruments and methodologies used to consolidate fragmented land in Germany and in the Netherlands.

Land consolidation is closely linked to a functioning land market. Indeed, one of the driving forces for land consolidation in many transitional countries is that land market, which provides an important instrument for both individuals and for the state. For the individuals it is to achieve better living standards and for the state, it is to provide income in the form of direct and indirect taxation. Sadjadi , stresses in Chapter 6 that the quality of the underlying legislation is the key element in developing an effective emerging land market. Normally the legislation is based upon a hierarchical structure, with the constitution being the highest and most important law to be followed. In this, the aims and ideals of the state will be defined, such as the fundamental rights of an individual to own private property. The constitution must also take into consideration any international treaties ratified by the state, and this is particularly important in the context of transnational agreements relating to

Introduction 3

the environment and sustainable development. In addition, Sadjadi gives examples of adjective and substantive aspects of legal instruments such as those influencing institutions, the environment, and the land. This latter aspect addresses such issues of inheritance law, fragmentation, and urban and rural development.

The generic theme of legal instruments relating to the land is given greater emphasis by Rognes and Sky in Chapter 7, where they address the specific issues of solving boundary disputes. This chapter provides an interesting overview of the problems of land consolidation but more specifically, describes the unique situation of Norway, with the land consolidation process being completely within the framework of the judicial system. One of the more important instruments used by land consolidation judges is mediation. Unlike most judges, the land consolidation judge is an expert on the substantive issues concerning boundary disputes and will often adjudicate decisions in the field rather than the court. Rognes and Sky also present an interesting study on the mediation behaviour of the land consolidation judges and arrive at the 'startling conclusion' that cases become immeasurably more complicated when lawyers represent their clients.

The next four chapters concern the problems related specifically to urban development. In contrast to the problems of boundary disputes, which normally take place in a rural environment, Groetalaers and Korthals Altes describe the policy instruments in the changing context of land development in the Netherlands. The Dutch municipalities have traditionally supplied land for development in the Netherlands. This process could typically involve a range of operations from drainage to the provision of services and associated infrastructure. As the result of recent changes, private land agents are now able to acquire land for development and this has had a great impact on the policy instruments used by the municipalities. Groetalaers and Korthals Altes make an interesting evaluation on the acquisition policy of land for development and, in particular, analyse the instruments used to acquire land. Although this chapter is specifically orientated towards the current situation in the Netherlands, it is, however a valuable appraisal of the problems that can be encountered in any country where there is a need to expand the living accommodation in and around urban areas.

This particular theme is also the subject of Chapter 9, in which Deakin examines the methodologies used to model the development of sustainable communities in close proximity to Edinburgh. In addition to this specific theme, Deakin also provides a good background to the legislative processes involved in the development of new settlements in Great Britain and more specifically, Scotland. One of the interesting aspects of this paper is the clearly defined, yet involved processes in the expansion of existing settlements, and the care taken not to destroy their unique character. This is a direct contrast to the 'new town' developments that took place in South East England during the 1960s, particularly the expansion of Bracknell and Basingstoke, which destroyed the character of the former settlements that have been enveloped by new developments.

Whereas the two proceeding chapters have primarily addressed the issues of development around existing settlements, Mutale in Chapter 10 examines the chronology and problems involved in a major urban redevelopment project, that of the

Railway Lands at King's Cross in London. The chapter provides a useful introduction to the British national planning framework and emphasises the relevance and importance of public participation at all levels of a redevelopment project. In addition to providing the spatial context of the urban redevelopment project, Mutale identifies and describes the inter-relationship between the actors, agendas, and processes involved in the project.

The fourth chapter on urban development describes the work of the BEQUEST(Building Environmental Quality Evaluation for Sustainability) network and the project's investigation into sustainable urban development. The methodology described by Deakin and Curwell should act as an exemplar for other networks. There are three main themes in this chapter; firstly developing a framework for a common understanding of urban sustainability, secondly, the development of a directory of environmental assessment methods, and thirdly, an analysis of the assessment methods developed by the network. Although a practical toolkit for of full assessment of sustainable urban development is still in the development process, a decision-support toolkit developed by BEQUEST will provide assistance to professions working in urban development.

The final two chapters examine specific methodologies used to model the parameters for rural and urban development. Both use Geographical Information Systems (GIS) as the basic tool for the analysis and display of the modelled spatial data. In Chapter 12, Adamu *et al.* introduce an object model to represent temporal changes in a GIS. The authors explore the nature of temporal GIS and the composite classes of a geographical object, together with their dynamic attributes. Such a model can be used to model sudden changes such as structural damage, as well as gradual changes such as flood events.

The application of GIS is continued by Yang Li *et al.* who use GIS techniques to evaluate community sustainability in forests in sub-Saharan Africa. In this chapter, they consider the different approaches to land use planning and evaluation that might be relevant and applicable to local people. The data acquired can then be represented as various land use, suitability, or cover polygons to provide indicators of open forest degradation. Finally, the model is applied to specific study area in Senegal, Tanzania, and Uganda.

Chapter 2

Partnership, Process, and Planning in Estuary Management: The Case of the Lower Thames

Robert Home

Introduction

The 1990s saw the rise of environmental issues up the public policy agenda, and a search for new methods of managing humanity's relationship with its environment. In 1992 the Earth Summit at Rio de Janeiro launched Local Agenda 21 as a means of involving local communities in environmental action. Meanwhile in the United Kingdom, the Environment Select Committee of the House of Commons identified a need for coastal and estuary zone protection, and planning (Environment Select Committee, 1992). Recognition of the human contribution to climate change has given an added urgency to the search for new approaches to estuary and coastal zone management (ECZM) (Agriculture Select Committee, 1998; DETR 2000).

Estuarial and coastal zones create particular challenges for management, policy and co-ordination, because of the juxtaposition of water and land, the relationship and often conflict of human activities, both with each other and with the natural environment, and in estuaries the transition from river to sea. Among the complex and inter-related issues are bio-diversity and water quality, commercial traffic and fisheries, physical dynamics and flood defences, land use planning and waterside development (Lee, 1993). ECZM extends beyond the role of local authorities, lacks statutory powers, and is affected an unusually diverse range of interests (Taussik, 1995).

The concept of partnership has emerged as a mechanism for co-operation particularly suited to ECZM. Among the legacies of Thatcherite free market ideology were a reluctance of government to create new statutory bodies, and consequently innovative approaches to co-operation between the public, private and community/voluntary sectors. The restructuring of, and resource constraints upon, local government generated a variety of partnership models involving stakeholders in an area. Competitive bidding, for example for City Challenge, Single Regeneration Budget and Lottery project funding, led to new-style, more inclusive partnerships to address regeneration priorities. New approaches to governance have included strengthening and restricting the statutory planning regime (through such measures as

6 *Methodologies, Models and Instruments*

the primacy of the statutory development plan, and restrictions upon the scope of material planning considerations), the emergence (or re-emergence) of non-statutory regional and sub-regional strategies and partnerships, and the increasing weight of European Union directives and measures (Thornley, 1993; Brindley, *et al.* 1996).

Partnership has now become:

> one of the most overused words in the language of governance, not least in the various policy arenas that comprise urban planning. Not surprisingly, the attraction of the term has depended partly on its vague and elastic meaning. Even the most cursory review of its use over the last two decades reveals widely varying mixes of public, private and voluntary agencies, operating at different spatial levels and levels of intensity (Ward, 1999).

Ward (1999) places partnerships in a fifty-year historical context, starting as primarily joint ventures between local authorities and private developers in town-centre development, but widening to the field of urban regeneration, and developing from essentially bilateral to multi-lateral relationships. The term can be seen as a rhetorical keyword, having no definitional consistency, but a number of available and developable meanings. It has also become a politically convenient substitute for more structured public sector interventions, at a time of ideological commitment to liberal, free-market, and inclusive alternatives to environmental issues.

Bailey (1995, pp.27-31) defined partnerships as:

> the mobilisation of a coalition of interests drawn from more than one sector in order to prepare and oversee an agreed strategy for the regeneration of a defined area.

He identified six types: development partnerships/joint ventures, development trusts, joint agreements/coalitions/companies, promotional partnerships (citing the East London Partnership as an example), agency partnerships (such as Urban Development Corporations), and strategic partnerships (such as sub-regional partnerships, citing the North Kent Forum). For Bailey crucial variables were the process of mobilisation, the range, and balance of power between the stakeholders, the nature and extent of the remit adopted, and the area of coverage. To these we might add the capacity to access or leverage resources, the transformational potential (changing or reconfiguring attitudes and relationships), outputs/achievements and their distributional impact (linked to an evaluation of effectiveness).

Estuary management represents a further extension of the partnership concept to address a complex eco-system affected by multiple interests and jurisdictions. The Thames Estuary Partnership (TEP) is attempting a new approach to partnerships, reflecting a limited statutory role, limited local authority involvement, and a wide range of potential partners, in an unusually complex political and environmental matrix.

Historical approaches to managing the Thames

The River Thames until the last quarter-century was seen, not as an endangered eco-system, but as a physical challenge, to be controlled, dredged, contained, bridged over and tunnelled beneath. Man has effected major changes to its physical form and dynamics, especially over the past two hundred years, so that the estuary bears little resemblance to the natural form that would have existed without human intervention. The river was (until the development of mass air travel) the main transport artery for the world city of London, bringing not just coals from Newcastle but the produce of Britain and the British Empire for processing and consumption. For the port of London changing transport technologies, particularly the increasing size of vessels and the construction of rail connections, created a restless process of dock and wharf construction, moving progressively down-river from the Pool of London to St. Katherine's Dock, the Isle of Dogs, the Royal group of docks (the largest area of impounded dock water in the world), and Tilbury and beyond (Astbury, 1980; Al Naib, 1996).

Until 1750, London Bridge was the only bridge across the seventy miles of the tidal Thames, but since then many bridges and tunnels have been constructed for road, rail and foot traffic. The Blackwall Tunnel, the first road tunnel under the river and in its time the largest underwater tunnel in the world, was opened in 1897. Tower Bridge (completed in 1894) was the furthest down-river bridge until the three road crossings at Dartford (two tunnels and a bridge) were built between 1963 and 1991, and the Channel Tunnel rail link is projected to cross near Dartford in the next decade. Various fixed crossings have been projected at Woolwich during the 20th century, but only a foot tunnel has so far been built to supplement the ferry.

Through the evolution of the public agencies responsible for the Thames, one can trace changing social and governmental perceptions of its role. Until the 19th century the Corporation of the City of London was the body responsible for the 'conservancy' of the Thames, but the growth in the size of vessels and volume of traffic using the river made that arrangement inadequate, and the City found itself in dispute with the Crown over matters of ownership and control. In 1857 the Thames Conservatory Act created a Board of Conservators, which in 1866 became the Thames Conservancy Board.

In the early 20th century government intervention sought to rationalise the organisation of the docks along the river and bring them under public control. A Royal Commission in 1902, found the port of London neglected, ill-equipped, inefficient, and in danger of losing much of its trade to other ports, both British and foreign, and was followed in 1909 by the creation of the Port of London Authority (the PLA): this combined the three remaining dock companies, took full control over the tidal river and its docking, dredged to the greater depths needed, and provided wider representation on its board. Two world wars and great changes in society and technology led to significant developments affecting the Thames estuary in the second half of the 20th century.

London's enclosed docks were extinguished in the space of less than 20 years, and the London Docklands Development Corporation (LDDC) embarked upon a

8   *Methodologies, Models and Instruments*

massive programme of regeneration in the 2200 hectares of redundant docks east of Tower Bridge on both sides of the Thames (Brownill, 1990). The Greater London Council (GLC) during its 21 years of existence (1965-86) built the Thames flood barrier (with government help), and in 1972 sought to extend its strategic role downriver with the holding of a Thameside Conference to explore the strategic possibilities of the vast acreage's of derelict land (where the Lakeside and Bluewater shopping centres were subsequently built).

Water quality improvements have been the statutory responsibility of three successive bodies in the last quarter century: the Thames Water Authority created in 1974, and succeeded, first by the National Rivers Authority, and then by the Environment Agency (the EA). Increased regulatory controls have contributed to a decline in polluting activities, improved water quality and changing ecological habitats.

From the late 1980s the East Thames Corridor, later rebadged as the Thames Gateway, became the focus of various sub-regional planning initiatives (Church, 1995; Home, 1999). The area's problems included de-industrialisation, lack of skills for the information technology economy, environmental degradation, and access. It contained large industrial plants, power stations and transmission lines, sewage treatment works, worked-out and working quarries, waste disposal sites, and railway yards (Serplan, 1987).

These changes in governance, and the growing public concern with environmental issues, combined to create a proliferation of initiatives and studies, and a political rediscovery of the Thames' role. Non-statutory bodies, such as the London Planning Advisory Committee, which came into existence in part to fill the gap in strategic planning left by the abolition of the Greater London Council (the GLC), offered models of how stake-holders could negotiate a consensus view of strategy, and hopefully establish a common language of discourse. The GLC in its last years produced the Thameside Guidelines, extending from East London to Rainham, and 'The Thames for Londoners - A Manifesto for the Use of the River' (GLC 1985; 1986). One of its successor agencies, the London Planning Advisory Committee, created a Thameside Working Party, and produced a set of 'guidelines' in 1990. The London Rivers Association was created in 1987, seeking to ensure that the Thames and London's other rivers were:

> integrated into the Capital's urban and social fabric through the maximisation of their economic, transport, amenity and ecological potential (LRA, 1992).

The Department of Transport created the River Thames Working Group in 1993 to maximise the transport use of the river. The following year the Thames Strategy, a study by consultants Ove Arup, was published, covering the river from Hampton Court to Greenwich. (GOL, 1995). At the same time the Thames Gateway sub-regional planning strategy was promoting the 'Lower Thames', down-river from the Thames Barrier, as a focus for future development activity. A planning study by consultants (Llewelyn-Davies, 1993) addressed a range of land-based development issues, while the Thames Gateway planning framework (later formalised as a sub-regional planning guidance in 1996) emphasised the environment and the potential of the river.

A new management approach to the Thames estuary

Into this fast-changing institutional and political environment English Nature launched the Thames Estuary Project in October 1992, as a flagship enterprise for the government's new 'Estuaries Initiative'. The United Kingdom has a quarter of the estuarine resources of Western Europe, and the Thames is the UK's most important estuary, extending from Tower Bridge in Greater London downstream to Shoeburyness on the north side and the Isle of Grain on the south side. While the English Nature team prepared a compilation of the main relevant legislation, primary roles and activities within the estuary, and data sources, 'key players' (land-owners, local authorities and other interest groups) were invited to prepare 'statements of interest', and 'topic groups' were assembled to report on a dozen agreed issues of interest (Kennedy, 1994; 1995).

In 1999 Project was renamed and reformed as the Thames Estuary Partnership, chaired by the Head of Planning and Environment at the Port of London Authority. The practical effects of the change was that the Thames Estuary Partnership (TEP) was established as a limited liability company (with charitable status), physically based at the Institute for Environmental Policy, within the Geography Department of University College London. The mechanics of the Partnership were a paid co-ordinator, steering group, and management group to deal with short-term issues. To raise the public profile of the TEP, a newsletter ('Talk of the Thames') and web-site (http://www.thamesweb.com/) were created, and an annual forum instituted, linked to an annual project audit. The launch of the partnership coincided with the publication of an 85-page document of management guidance (Thames Estuary Partnership, 1999), listing nearly two hundred organisations as contributing, and identifying 13 'themes' and 101 'principles for action'. An action plan listed some 130 potential projects over a 15-year agenda.

The language and style of the management guidance reflected the voluntary and inclusive style of the Partnership:

> culture of openness and communication ... a chance to work within the bigger picture ... a detailed overview of the key estuarine themes ... highlight issues and opportunities.

The attempt to balance different and often conflicting interests is reflected in the broadly defined 'vision' statement as:

> an estuary which is valued and appreciated as a place to live, work and relax, an environmental asset and a focus for economic growth (p2).

While an individual statutory agency might have 'policies' and even a 'plan', a loose-fit partnership had to adopt a more consensual language of 'management guidance' and 'principles for action'. In the words of the preface:

Methodologies, Models and Instruments

to ensure that the right balance is struck between social, economic and environmental considerations in taking forward the concept of sustainable development.

Notwithstanding the non-statutory status of the TEP, the language of governance, officialdom and statutory planning influenced the management guidance, reflected in phrases like 'ensure consistency with' and 'responsive to the needs of the local community', and in the relatively formal processes of public consultation and successive draft documents.

The TEP is an attempt to treat the estuary as a single unit across many interests and organisational boundaries. The local government authorities, which had statutory planning powers over development plan-making and development control, were in some areas two-tier (county and district), in others unitary, while the new arrangements for London government created a further complication. The EA had statutory powers for regulating waste disposal to land, industrial releases to air, and safeguarding and improving the natural water environment. Local communities, the private sector, landowners, and voluntary sector were involved.

Inevitably the politics and agendas of these different partners affected the development of the partnership. In the early years the lead co-ordinating role was from English Nature, but it was seen by many to have a bias towards environmental protection. The offer of a physical home with the Geography Department of University College London was partly because an academic institution was seen as neutral, although it was inevitably concerned with identifying research projects for funding applications. The EA had a major stake, seconding a staff member to work on the biodiversity aspect, and, with its programme of preparing Local Environment Agency Plans (LEAPs). These five-year action programmes in air quality, water resources, and bio-diversity followed a Local Agenda 21 commitment by its predecessor, the NRA, and LEAP approach was applied to the management guidance in the sections on air quality, bio-diversity, waste, flood defence and clean water. The Port of London Authority provided the partnership chairman, and was concerned with raising the profile of the river as a commercial transport route.

A research forum was held in September 2000, attended by about a hundred researchers, and explored possible research directions through sub-groups on biodiversity, fisheries, planning and environment, flood defence/physical dynamics, and water quality. The academic community's interest in the TEP was reflected in an intellectual debate over its cross-disciplinary possibilities for an 'open and iterative dialogue'. One research approach was eco-system management, derived from American experience with the Great Lakes. This views an estuary as a complex inter-action of habitats, with humans as 'sentinel species' as the top of the food chain, and comprehensive management should recognise the inter-relationships of land, water, air and living things (including humans) (Attrill, 2000).

The integrated approach to estuary management was based upon the concept of post-normal science (Funtowicz and Ravetz, 1993), recognising the combination of uncertainty and high decision stakes, and encouraging:

a reflexive dialogue between social and natural scientists that works towards integrating the technical (i.e. scientific and economic) with the contextual (e.g. social concerns).

Post-normal science encourages multiple approaches to problems and accepts those scientific facts and social values are related. It respects that the problems are created and a broader extended peer community evaluates solutions. Science works within this arena to provide scientific inputs or forecasts that serve as inputs to the decision-making process... In the case of rising sea levels, current predictions of sea level rise, based on simplistic models often calibrated by relatively 'soft' data, will be used to guide management plans, yet our knowledge is very uncertain. However, to ignore the potential risks posed by predicted sea level rises would almost certainly result in more dire consequences in the long run. Because post-normal science accepts the uncertain nature of scientific information and the interconnectedness of scientific 'facts' and social 'values', it is an appropriate form of science where the knowledge is uncertain, decisions are urgent and stakes are high, such as in the Thames Estuary (Motiuk, 2000).

Such an approach also has to recognise the conflicts of interest involved in ECZM.

Conflicts in estuary management

The TEP has hitherto intervened little in conflict situations, and has resisted being a consultee to the many statutory development plan reviews within the area. A partnership based upon consensus shies away from conflict, yet conflicts and pressures upon the estuary are inevitable. Three examples of potential conflict can be cited: between development pressures and environmental protection, between commercial interests and public access to the riverside, and between flood defence and property rights.

The first conflict (development or environment) lies at the heart of the land use planning system. Estuaries are favoured locations for human settlement, which places additional pressures upon the eco-system. The potential conflict between development pressures and environmental protection is best symbolised by the existence of the Thames Gateway London Partnership to redirect new development towards east London and the lower Thames (Church, 1995). Much of this development will be on the waterfront, conflicting with environmental protection. The alluvial mud of the estuary covers many archaeological remains reflecting the commercial importance of the river over centuries, such as timber trackways, wrecks, fish-traps, military installations, and provides one of the most important winter feeding areas in Europe for wildfowl and wading birds, with large areas designated for statutory and international protection. The mosaic of habitats comprises mudflats (offering rich invertebrate feeding grounds for wildfowl), shingle, intertidal vegetation, and grazing marshes and wasteland.

The second conflict is between the commercial uses of the river and the demand for public access to the waterfront for recreation. The Port of London is the largest in the UK, receiving cargo of aggregates, cement, fuels, containers, dry bulk goods for food processing (sugar, rice, and grain) and waste. The PLA, unlike other ports, owns little land itself, and depends upon partnership to realise the growth potential of port-related development. The limited number of sites suitable for port development (offering deep sheltered water, flat topography and good land access) have received little long-term safeguarding from the planning system, so that many have been lost to other development in recent decades (LRA, 1994). Refuse disposal is the largest intra-port traffic on the Thames, yet new environmental standards are making planning consents harder to obtain. Such riparian industrial and commercial land uses compete with the public pressure to walk along the riverbank and to use the water for fishing, boating and leisure. Planning guidance has sought to set back riverside development to allow public access between development and the river, and has proposed the concepts of focal points along the river (with public art, planting or lighting), and 'permeable' riverside development (allowing, in planner-speak, visual and pedestrian interlinkage with the hinterland). The Countryside Commission pioneered the Thames Path (opened in 1996) from its source to the Thames Barrier, but pedestrian accessibility to riverside remains poor east of Greenwich. The industrialised stretches of the lower Thames make the creation of continuous walkways unlikely, although circular walks linking the hinterland with the river have been devised.

A third area of conflict is between landowners and flood protection strategies. The Thames represents some 75% of the country's property at potential flood risk (400,000 properties with an estimated total value of £150 billion), yet little recent research has been undertaken on its morphology and physical processes, particularly on reducing tidal levels and maintaining estuary stability. After the 1953 floods, it was argued that a bad repetition could potentially affect an area as great as 45 square miles, overwhelming over a million people and quarter of a million buildings in central London, as well as paralysing underground services. The Thames Barrier and Flood Prevention Act was passed in 1972, and the barrier completed in 1982, just upstream from the Woolwich Ferry. The capital cost of £500 million was contributed, 75 per cent by central government, and the rest by the Greater London Council, and the barrier was designed to protect the capital against a flood return period of 1 in 1000 years up to the year 2030. Recent researchers have advocated managed retreat from rising sea levels, and the setting aside of 'sacrificial land', which can be lost to the waters. However, the pressure from property owners for expensive flood prevention measures can only increase, as the response to the wide-ranging floods of the autumn of 2000 has shown.

Conclusions

The Thames Estuary Partnership has developed since 1993 as a response to the newly perceived and complex challenges of estuary and coastal zone management. Returning to the three keywords adopted in the title of this paper, and drawing upon the analytical framework in Bailey (1995), we can now assess the TEP as a partnership, a process, and a planning mechanism.

The partnership concept evolved to bring together a variety of stakeholders (national agencies, local authorities and communities, landowners and the private

Partnership, Process, and Planning in Estuary Management

sector, and voluntary groups) in a co-ordinated approach to issues of common concern. It become a device for articulating projects and marshalling resources for urban development and regeneration, particularly in the competitive bidding environment of the Single Regeneration Budget, the Lottery and the funding programmes which preceded them. The TEP represents an expansion of the concept to embrace a significantly wider spread of partners, a wider geographical area, and complex ecosystems and environmental processes. It has some similarities with the sub-regional partnerships which emerged in the 1990s (Thames Gateway London being a nearby example), but is addressing issues of unusual range and complexity. The core partners are the Environment Agency, the PLA, and the academic research community (led by the Geography Department of University College London), but the interested groups cover a spectrum from single-issue lobby groups to local authorities with multiple statutory functions and political responsibilities. The emphasis upon a voluntary and consensual style disguises often conflicting agendas, but the partnership offers a vehicle for raising awareness, developing a common discourse and commitment, and capturing resources, and thus represents a new evolution in the linkage between public, private and community sectors.

Viewed as a process, the TEP is still evolving, some seven years after its inception as the Thames Estuary Project, and has no set time-scale for its activities. In the preparation of management guidance, it has borrowed heavily from the formalised process of statutory plan making. With such characteristics as wide consultation and awareness-raising, the formulation of a draft document modified by an iterative procedure, written consensual principles for action negotiated between the parties, in-built flexibility recognising a changing external context, issue-specific groups, and periodic review and audit. The non-statutory remit of the partnership required a voluntary co-operative approach, with 'the Thames estuary community' assembled at an annual forum to review progress and identify new issues and opportunities.

Evaluating the TEP as a planning mechanism, one should first acknowledge its lack of statutory backing or funding, and its existence outside or alongside the statutory machinery for land use planning. It is, therefore, appropriate to apply a flexible or layman's definition of planning: devising a scheme of action, or a method or way of proceeding. It has taken about six years (a similar period to that needed for statutory plan preparation) to devise, not such much a plan of action, but a set of management guidelines, and an agreed list of a hundred potential projects (some of them already completed or under way). The aims set out in the management guidelines are more general rather than specific, avoiding targets for achievement, but this does not prevent an evaluation of the effectiveness or achievements of the TEP to date. Any estuary represents a complex ecosystem, where human interventions may have long-term environmental effects. Our understanding of the complex interactions and physical dynamics within the estuary is limited, so it seems appropriate that the next phase in the TEP will largely comprise research of a 'post-normal' kind, which recognises the uncertainties of both the environment and the decision-making context.

As a consensual association of interests, the TEP is unlikely to take sides in conflict situations, but it may find it opposing large-scale interventions in the estuary eco-system, for instance resisting waterfront development, which jeopardises

14 *Methodologies, Models and Instruments*

environmental interests. As climate instability increases flood risk and threatens the effectiveness of the Thames Barrier, then the need to safeguard London may soon inject a greater sense of urgency and resources into the work of the TEP, and into the agencies with the main statutory responsibilities for the river, i.e. the EA and the PLA. When major national interests and private capital are involved, the TEP may yet find itself side-lined, or, while it has not yet sought any significant advocacy role, might yet find such a role forced upon it.

An initiative such as the TEP, concerned with a major ecosystem and complex natural processes operating over long time-scales, should be evaluated over a longer time-scale than projects with more specific objectives and planned interventions. So far the TEP has represented an imaginative approach, seeking to involve interests as diverse as the estuary itself. Its main achievement to date has been a statement of management guidelines, not involving any parties in major resource commitments or difficult decisions. What will happen when the stakes get higher, and the conflicts inherent in the situation (particularly between political priorities, private profit, and environmental protection) become sharper and more visible? A major natural disaster, the most obvious being a flood of the Thames, may test the effectiveness of the TEP as an instrument for estuary management.

References

Agriculture Select Committee, 1998. *Flood and Coastal Defence*, 6th Report, Session 1997-98, London.

Al Naib, S.K., 1996. *London Docklands: Past, Present and Future*, (7th Ed.), Research Books, Romford.

Astbury, A.K., 1980. *Estuary: Land and Water in the Lower Thames Basin*, Carnforth Press, London.

Attrill, M., 2000. *The Ecosystem Approach: Making the Linkages*, Thames Estuary Research Forum, London.

Bailey, N., 1995. *Partnership Agencies in British Urban Policy*, UCL Press, London.

Brindley, T., *et al.*, 1996. *Remaking Planning: The Politics of Urban Change*, Routledge, London.

Brownill, S., 1990. *Developing London's Docklands: Another Great Planning Disaster*, Paul Chapman, London.

Church, A. and Frost, M., 1995. The Thames Gateway - an Analysis of the Emergence of a sub-regional Regeneration Perspective. *Geographical Journal*, **161**(2), 199-209.

DETR, 2000. *Development and Flood Risk: PPG 25*, DETR, London.

Environment Select Committee, 1992. *CZ Protection and Planning*, House of Commons 2nd Report.

Funtowicz, S.O. and Ravetz, J.R., 1993. Science for the post-normal age, *Futures*, **25**(7), 739-756.

GOL, 1995. *Thames Strategy*, Government Regional Office for London, DoE, London.

Home, R.K., 1999. Sustainable development in the Thames Gateway. In: Dixon-Gough, R.W. (ed.), *Land Reform and Sustainable Development*, Ashgate, Aldershot, 278-288.

Kennedy, K., 1994. *Issues on the North Thames - a Case for Estuary Management*, English Nature, London.

Kennedy, K., 1995. Producing management plans for major estuaries - the need for a systematic approach: a case study of the Thames Estuary. In: Healey, M.G. and Doody, J.P., (eds.), *Directions in European Coastal Management*, Samara, Cardigan, 451-459.

Lee, E., 1993. The political ecology of coastal planning and management in England and Wales: policy responses to the implications of sea level rise, *Geographical Journal*, **159**, 169-78.

Llewelyn-Davies, 1993. *East Thames Corridor: A Study of Development Capacity and Potential*, Department of the Environment, HMSO, London.

LRA, 1992. *The Working Thames: An Agenda for Action*, London Rivers Association, London.

LRA, 1994. *Key Industrial Sites on River Thames Lost over Last Five Years*, London Rivers Association, London.

Motiuk, L., 2000. In situ Science: an Analysis of Where Science Sits. In: *Integrated Estuarine Management*, Thames Estuary Research Forum, London.

Serplan, 1987. *Development Potential in the Eastern Thames Corridor, RCP700*, Serplan, London.

Taussik, J., 1995. The contribution of development plans to coastal policy. In: Healey, M.G. and Doody, J.P. (eds.), *Directions in European Coastal Management*, Samara, Cardigan.

Thames Estuary Partnership, 1999. *Management Guidance for the Thames Estuary: Today's Estuary for Tomorrow*, Thames Estuary Partnership, London.

Thornley, A., 1993. *Urban Planning Under Thatcherism: The Challenge of the Market*, Routledge, London.

Ward, S.V., 1999. Public-private partnerships. In: Cullingworth, B., (ed.), *British Planning: 50 Years of Urban and Regional Policy*, Athlone, London and New Brunswick, N.J., 232-249.

Chapter 3

Land Reform in Developing Countries: Legal and Institutional Aspects

Alec McEwen

Introduction

Proposals for land reform in developing countries often pose two basic questions. First, should any land be capable of private ownership, or should the state retain the legal ownership of all land, subject to specified rights of use and occupancy by those individual persons or groups of person to whom the state may grant such rights? Second, how can the state best identify the location, size, and characteristics of every land parcel, whether publicly or privately owned, and the legal rights that affect it, as part of a national land information system?

The availability of powerful tools such as GPS, GIS, and remote sensing, may encourage a belief that problems of land reform are susceptible largely to technological solution. However, technology, even when judiciously applied, is not enough. There must also be an appropriate legal framework, an adequate institutional infrastructure, and sufficient financial support that will ensure both the viability and sustainability of the reform.

Land ownership or land use

'Property is theft', protested the French philosopher Pierre-Joseph Proudhon in 1840. A half-century earlier the English agriculturalist Arthur Young declared, 'The magic of property turns sand to gold'. This apparent contradiction is reflected in the modern world where some countries take for granted the right of an individual person to own a parcel of land, while other countries insist that all their land belongs to the state.

Even in capitalist societies, a distinction may be found between land ownership and land use. For example, in their early treaties with European settlers the aboriginal peoples of Canada regarded land not as a marketable commodity but as a resource to be shared. In their view, land 'ownership' means land use, not an exclusive personal title to the soil. In Canada's more than 2,500 reserves, where the federal Crown holds the legal title to the land on behalf of the Indian bands (or First Nations as they prefer to be called), an individual person cannot acquire outright private ownership. The highest form of available title is a Certificate of

Land Reform in Developing Countries

Possession, which can, however, pass by inheritance (McEwen, 1992). The same unavailability of individual private ownership applies in those areas of Canada's vast northern territories that are held collectively by Inuit and by Indian aboriginal nations under fee simple title. A similar situation exists in Alberta where the Métis hold their only Canadian land base under a collective fee simple title (McEwen, 1995).

The individual ownership of surface rights to land normally includes all buildings, structures, and other objects that are attached to the soil. In other words, it comprises all those features that are classed as immovable property under a civil code system and as real property under common law. Zanzibar provides an interesting exception to this general rule, for its Land Tenure Act provides that economic trees, such as clove and coconut, can be owned separately from a right of ownership or occupancy of the land. Indeed, any one tree may have a large number of co-owners, each with an undivided interest, and it can pass by inheritance. It is possible that those co-owners own none of the land containing the tree, not even excepting the portion of the ground in which its roots are planted.

Equally noteworthy are those jurisdictions where a person may own a house or other building but not the land on which it sits. In such situations the state retains ownership of the land but grants a right of occupancy under specified conditions that usually include the purpose for which the land must be used, the duration of the right, and the rental or other fee that is payable. One effect of this arrangement is the creation of two registration systems, separately administered, one for buildings, and the other for land. The notion of a unified registerable title is an alien concept.

In Mongolia, buildings are registered in the decentralised State Immovable Property Registry (SIPR) which is part of the Ministry of Justice. This is really a misnomer, for that institution does not register land, even though the Mongolian Civil Code includes land within its definition of immovable property. Nor does registration extend to buildings owned by the state; it applies only to private houses and apartment units. The *ger*, a portable, circular, tent-like dwelling favoured by nomadic herders, is regarded as movable property because it is not fixed to the soil. But in urban areas, particularly in the capital city of Ulaanbaatar, where there may be as many as 80,000 *gers*, these residences have assumed a more permanent character and some of them are registered in the SIPR. Parcels of land for individual use and occupancy are allocated by the local municipal authority, which issues a certificate to each successful applicant. Details of these certificates are registered with the decentralised Land Administration Authority of the Ministry for Nature and Environment. The Mongolian Land Law states that the possession for allocated land may be for an initial period of 60 years, with a one-time extension of not more than 40 years. The ostensible duration of 100 years prompts some government officials to assert that since it is, in effect, equivalent to ownership, land privatisation is unnecessary. In practice, the initial period may be 15 years or even less, the actual term depending on the discretion of the land-allocating authority. Proposed amendments to the Land Law include allowing allocated land rights to be transferred to third parties by sale or gift and to permit the land to be mortgaged as security for a loan (UB Post, 2000). This proposal may be inspired, at least in part, by the official recognition that land rights are sold from time to time on the informal market, despite the present illegality of such transactions.

Resistance to land privatisation does not always rest solely on political ideology; it may be influenced by practical concerns. The Ukraine Land Code of 1992 ended the state monopoly of land and recognised three forms of ownership: state, collective, and private. Yet the replacement of collective farms by private agricultural enterprises in which individual peasants hold land-share rights brings new problems. Although land rights can be lawfully sold, exchanged, or used as collateral, selling a land share is complicated and expensive. Nor can shares be merged to create a bigger holding. In fact, farm output has shrunk every year since 1991 (*Economist*, 1999). The breaking up of collective farms in the Russian Federation, upon the recommendation of perhaps over-zealous foreign advisers, contributed to the collapse of many farms and fostered sceptical attitudes towards the professed advantages of private ownership (*Globe and Mail*, 2000). Similar doubts arose in Moldova and Uzbekistan where many local experts believe that the unrestricted privatisation of rural land will lead inevitably to loss of agricultural production. Ideological objections may also include the view that the occupation and use of land is a form of stewardship from which all members of society, not just the occupant of the land parcel, should benefit. It could be argued, for example, that the private owner of an unimproved parcel should not reap the reward of its increased value caused by urban development, not by the owner's own efforts. In some cities of the People's Republic of China the owner who sells his or her privatised residential apartment must share any profit from the sale with the work unit from which the apartment was originally purchased (*Economist*, 2000).

Land law

Laws relating to land in developing countries should reflect both customary practices and the will of the people as expressed in legislation that is interpreted and applied by the courts and enforced by the administering authority. Written laws typically consist of relevant articles of the Constitution and the Civil Code (in civil law systems), supplemented by a number of acts, regulations, and orders that deal with particular areas of land management and administration. As a pre-condition of providing funds for a land reform project under a loan agreement, the donor organisation often requires the recipient government to enact specified pieces of legislation, which might include laws governing land adjudication, land tribunal and land title registration. Unfortunately, the prompt passage of legislation in response to this requirement carries no assurance as to its suitability for the project's intended purpose.

The drafting of legislation involves more than the legal scrivener's art. New or amended laws must reflect government policy. However, they must also be capable of implementation, a consideration that presupposes an adequate institutional infrastructure and a sufficiency of human and other resources to undertake the project. Not only must the project itself be viable, it must also be

Land Reform in Developing Countries 19

sustainable by the implementing agency, even if no additional outside funding is likely to be available to continue or complete the work. Where project funds come mainly from a loan that must be repaid, even over a long period of time and under generous terms, the borrower's ability to generate revenue to meet that repayment may be a factor in deciding whether or not to proceed with the project at all.

Changes of government may represent shifts in policy that render existing or proposed legislation inappropriate. In Canada, the three provinces of New Brunswick, Nova Scotia and Prince Edward Island each passed a Land Titles Act in the 1970s. Except in New Brunswick, where the law was proclaimed only with respect to a pilot project in one county, the legislation has not been brought into force. In the two other provinces, the laws lie in a legal limbo where they may eventually be repealed or simply omitted from a future consolidation of the statutes.

In the year 2000 Trinidad and Tobago, in compliance with the terms of a loan agreement, enacted three new laws: Land Adjudication Act, Land Tribunal Act and Registration of Titles to Land Act. At the time of writing, none of these laws has been proclaimed in force. An earlier enactment, the Land Registration Act of 1981, never came into operation. It seems reasonable to predict that the new legislation will not take effect until the necessary institutional and financial resources are provided. Should the Registration of Titles to Land Act be proclaimed that Trinidad and Tobago will have three different systems to record the ownership of, and the legal interests in, land? The two laws currently in force are the Real Property Ordinance, which is Torrens-type legislation introduced in 1895 but now little used, and the Registration of Deeds Act, dating from 1885, which is essentially a repository of documents that may or may not be evidence of title.

A comparative analysis of land legislation in other jurisdictions can assist a developing country in enacting its own laws. Yet the object should be to find solutions that are based solely on local needs and circumstances. The uncritical adoption of legislation that appears to operate satisfactorily under different conditions elsewhere may lead to a Procrustean conformity that proves unworkable in the country of its reception.

Peru provides an example of well-intentioned legislation that created a land titles registration system, which despite its successful introduction, falls short of assuring the certainty of title which that system is expected to offer. Registration of title normally implies that, subject to specified overriding interests, all legal transactions affecting the registered parcel, such as a sale or a mortgage, must themselves be registered to have legal validity. Unfortunately, this is not a requirement with respect to titles registered in the Urban Property Registry (RPU). Under current Peruvian law, the holder of the registered title to a parcel may transfer or encumber the parcel without any requirement to register the transfer or encumbrance. Since the registration of legal transactions affecting registered title is a voluntary act, it can be readily appreciated that unless there is a legal obligation to register all such transactions subsequent to initial registration, the registry itself will lose its integrity. In the course of time, the recorded information will become incomplete and unreliable, thus destroying the very purpose for which the registry was originally created. The Peruvian officials who administer the RPU are not unaware of this problem, which is due in part to the unwillingness of transacting parties to pay the required registration fees.

Institutions

The implementation of a land reform project in a developing country assumes the availability of a local institution that has sufficient capability and resources either to perform the work itself or to support a separate project team. Where two or more local institutions have responsibility for implementing the project, it is essential to identify their respective roles and duties. Failure to settle this issue may lead to ministerial turf wars and lack of interdepartmental co-operation.

No less important is the need to harmonise the project with other similar projects that are being undertaken. In Peru, two separate organisations, each supported by a different donor, are engaged in issuing land titles. The Commission for the Formalisation of Informal Titles (COFOPRI) deals mainly with the problem of urban squatters, while the Special Project for Rural Land Titling and Cadastre (PETT) has a somewhat similar function in the rural areas. Both organisations would benefit from their adoption of common standards and procedures relating, for example, to air photography, map scales, and the verification process needed to justify the issuance of individual titles.

Wherever possible, the local institution should keep members of the public informed of the purpose and progress of the project. This is particularly desirable in projects involving cadastral survey and land registration, which some landowners may see as nothing more than the prelude to increased taxation. The process of land adjudication will be facilitated if its object is explained in terms that are easy to understand, by means of public meetings, radio, and television broadcasts, and print media. An imaginative approach in Zanzibar produced an excellent video in 1995 entitled, 'A New System of Land Registration', performed enthusiastically by local amateur actors, the script of which was also adapted for radio. In 1996, a cadastral project in Moldova engaged a public relations consultant to present a weekly radio broadcast that discussed the work and invited questions and comments from the public.

The implementing institution should also keep local professional associations informed of the project and its possible implications for their members. Proposed changes from a deeds-recording system to a land titles system, for example, may create fear among notaries that the replacement of arcane, prolix deeds of conveyance by simple certificates of title will result in their loss of income. Such concerns can be allayed by showing notaries how the new system can benefit their work and by pointing out that prudent purchasers and mortgagees should still seek legal services to determine the possible existence of overriding interests and other unregistered encumbrances before entering into transactions.

Because of their laws protecting state secrets, some governments restrict the availability of vital information, even when it is required for a project from which their nation will benefit. Topographic maps at a scale larger than, say, 1:500 000

Land Reform in Developing Countries 21

may be unavailable except to a few designated institutions and the co-ordinate values of geodetic survey control points may be inaccessible. A pilot cadastral project undertaken in western Ukraine in 1993-96 was obliged to use false co-ordinates despite the equal participation in the project of the very government agency that generates national geodetic co-ordinate information. Overcoming problems of this nature may require a prior commitment by the local authorities that they will release maps and survey data essential to the project.

In countries where land was neither privatised nor taxed, the expression 'cadastral survey' signified a land inventory that recorded land characteristics including, for example, the fertility, humus content and pollution of the soil, the type of vegetation cover and the actual or potential land use. The move toward private land ownership, on which a rent or tax is levied, compels the need for a legal and a fiscal cadastre as well. It is important to identify these three cadastral components and to assign their administration to the appropriate institution. The Cadastral Mapping and Survey Law of Mongolia, which came into force on 1st January 2000 but is not yet in operation, contains provisions relating to all three types of cadastre, without clearly distinguishing each one, and might suggest that they should all be the responsibility of a single institution.

Before the establishment of a national land information system (NLIS) can be contemplated, it is necessary to decide what form the system is to take and how it will be administered. The existing cadastral framework can provide a useful base for an NLIS, but in areas that have no such framework the system may have to be constructed from the available survey data, cartography, and topographic information. One administrative possibility is the creation of a single agency, which stores, maintains and disseminates various types of land information. An Alberta example of this kind is the Spatial Data Warehouse, sponsored by government and private industry, that maintains, updates, manages and markets provincial cadastral, topographic and related digital data. Another possibility is the creation or designation of an agency whose primary function is to co-ordinate the activities of the existing organisations that collect data, without requiring them to lose control over that information. In selecting the administrative mechanism, the emphasis should be on ensuring that land information is accessible to all legitimate users on a timely basis.

Technology

It is tempting to be dazzled by the almost overwhelming array of technology that is available to assist in the realisation of land reform projects. The selection of a technological application for a project must consider several factors: equipment costs, availability of trained operators, maintenance questions and overall suitability. The mere computerisation of land records, for example, may be insufficient unless the underlying problems of the system are rectified. It may be reactionary, even heretical to argue for the retention of a manual system, that satisfies local users. Yet an outside observer may discover in a developing country

22 *Methodologies, Models and Instruments*

a manual system that works well in practice even though it is not supposed to work in theory.

A possible combination of various types of technology may be advisable. In a large, lightly-populated country like Mongolia, where one-third of its people live in the capital city, it would be wasteful and inefficient to contemplate large-scale, conventional line mapping for all areas, including those that are remote and virtually uninhabited. Urban areas lend themselves to softcopy orthophoto imagery from which scalable information is obtainable in digital format. Croplands and pastures could be mapped by satellite imagery to a positional accuracy of between 10 and 30 metres, which should be sufficient for most land management purposes.

The Global Positioning System (GPS) offers a technique that has revolutionised surveying practice, though its application to cadastral surveys has yet to be fully exploited in some countries. In Trinidad and Tobago the State Land (Regularisation of Tenure) Act, 1998 protects existing squatters on public land from ejectment and facilitates their acquisition of leasehold titles. Since the first step includes issuing each squatter with a Certificate of Comfort, some simple but reasonably accurate method of locating the occupied parcel is required. In the absence of recent air photography or large-scale maps of the squatter areas, the administering authority on the Island of Trinidad is considering using GPS to identify the location of the parcels, many of which are scattered. Until recently single-point GPS, positioning could be expected to yield about 100-metre accuracy. The termination of Selective Availability (under which satellite clock and orbit information contained an intentional error) by the United States Department of Defence in May 2000 now improves the accuracy of single-point positioning to about 30 metres, which might be adequate for many cadastral requirements. Much greater accuracy can be obtained by using the differential method in which a second GPS receiver at a station of known position maintains observations throughout the survey.

Surveys of urban areas, where high land values may demand greater precision of measurement, can be efficiently undertaken with the aid of electronic instruments such as the Total Station, which records both angles and distances. This type of equipment may be too costly to justify its use in rural areas. In some countries local land managers still measure the boundaries of allocated agricultural parcels crudely but sufficiently accurately by rolling a graduated perambulator wheel or by walking the two legs of a hinged rod that open to a fixed distance apart of, say, two metres.

Conclusion

Although technology can contribute importantly to the solution of land reform problems its application may be of limited effect unless the necessary legislation and institutional infrastructure are in place. The initial steps towards the implementation of a land registration project, for example, often include air photography, ground control, and cadastral mapping. All three activities are relatively straightforward operations because they do not usually require new laws to carry them out. Nor need members of the public be directly affected by this work; indeed, they may remain unaware that it is being undertaken. But once the project completes its cadastral base maps it moves into the murkier area of individual property rights in which legislation for land adjudication and the registration of titles has a considerable social and economic impact. Not everyone would accept W.S. Gilbert's contention that, 'The law is the true embodiment of everything that's excellent'. It is easier to agree with Alexander Pope that, 'Whate'er is best administer'd is best'. However, appropriate laws and institutions will always be crucial to the success of land reform.

References

Economist, 1999. Unreformed, 11th September.
Economist, 2000. Housing's great leap forward, 30th September.
Globe and Mail, 2000. Betting the farm - and losing, Toronto, 19th January.
McEwen, A., 1992. Land holding and boundary surveys on Indian Reserves in Canada. In: *Proceedings of the International Conference on Cadastral Reform, Department of Surveying and Land Information*, University of Melbourne.
McEwen, A., 1995. The Metis settlements land registry in Alberta, *Survey Review*, **33**(256), 77-86.
UB Post, 2000. *Land 'Ownership' Draws Near*, Ulaanbaatar, 9th November.

Chapter 4

International Land Management: Aspects on Education and Training

Reinfried Mansberger and Erwin Heine

Introduction

> Knowledge is one of the most important resources for high-industrialised countries and education and training are the fundamental ingredients for the development process of this resource (Hartermann, 1999).

The responsibility for the resource 'Knowledge' lies in the hands of politicians, governments, administrative bodies, research organisations, and education institutions. Research organisations and education institutions have to prepare and to provide high-quality education and up-to-date training for junior experts in the specific professions. They also have to care for continuing professional development (life-long learning). Politicians and governments are obliged to provide frame conditions to impart knowledge and to mobilise capital for scientific education and training programmes. Finally administrative bodies have to co-ordinate the education institutions, and to monitor the content and quality of training courses.

The above-mentioned statement of Hartermann (1999) must be extended: knowledge is not only one of the most important resources for high-industrialised countries but it is an essential resource all over the globe. The globalisation of economy and the complexity of global ecology demand well-educated experts in every country and in every region of the earth. The high-industrialised countries have met this need within the last decades: Consulting services, education and training became substantial export articles to developing countries.

Research and educational bodies always are forced to scrutinise occupational areas, and they have to adapt their course programmes to the demands of the specific fields of professions, regarding also the specific needs of different countries.

International land management is a complex discipline that requires knowledge in the field of ecology, economy, jurisprudence, sociology, and technology. In a world with a rapid pace of change, the development of professionals has to respond quickly to changing market conditions, to client requirements, and to the influences of government policies (FIG, 1999). All those involved in the education and training of land managers, have to stay abreast of the extra skills required and should be capable of ensuring the growth of the knowledge resource essential to the field of land administration and land information.

The chapter focuses on the profession of land managers in general and on educational and training issues in particular. It illustrates the demands for this profession, outlines unanswered questions in education, and addresses current activities on continuing professional development.

The renaissance of land management

Some decades ago Land Register (in the meaning of Land Books and Land Cadastre), Land Reform, and Land Development were regarded as a dead-end-street in education and in the field activity of surveyors. Keywords such as Geographic Information Systems (GIS), Global Positioning Systems (GPS), Inertial Navigation Systems (INS), and Location Based Services (LBS) were the eye-catchers for the surveying education during the last two decades.

However, times change and the *three-character activities* identified above are still important in all education and training programmes for surveyors, although an increasing trend can be recognised that other professions and other educational courses use these new technologies as tools for thematic data acquisition and data management. Furthermore, one does not necessarily need to be a prophet to foresee that within the next twenty years, the surveyors will lose the hegemony for these methods through the ease of handling of both the instruments and systems.

The importance of land administration, land reform, land consolidation, and land development, which are summarised by the term land management, has increased dramatically during the last decade. The reasons for this apparent renaissance are to be found in the:

- decrease of natural resources and the necessity of an economical use of them;
- expansion of living space, exemplified by the increase of global population and the finiteness of land for urban expansion, need controlled planning and good fundamental spatial data;
- inter-relationship between of agribusiness and ecologically compatible agriculture, which should not be a contradiction. Nevertheless, economic food production and sustainability of nature are based on carefully formulated, land development plans; and the
- collapse of communism together with the shift of many countries towards market-driven economies that requires a good system of land documentation.

Figure 4.1 illustrates the range of organisations in the United Kingdom involved in land information, an essential part of land management. The high number of institutions involved and activities indicated is a measure of the level of manpower needed in national land management. However, at an international level the demand for land managers is also increasing: Investigators or credit grantors, as European Union (EU), United Nations (UN) or World Bank (WB) force those countries that are requesting financial aid to fulfil the principles of good governance (Magel, 2000; Creuzer, 2000). Furthermore, amongst these principles are security of rights, safety of property, efficient administration - or in other words, a functioning land management system.

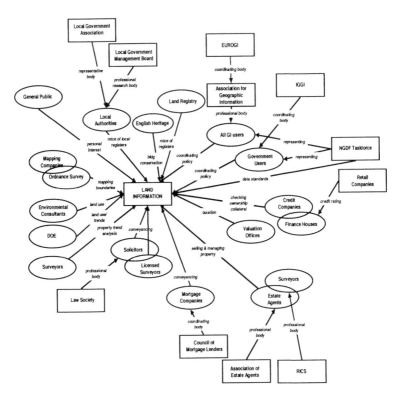

Figure 4.1   Organisations in the UK involved with land information
Source: MADAME (2000) (Methods for Access to Data and Metadata in Europe)

Job Specification

The increasing importance of land management and the need for experts to meet the new requirements of land administration and land development is a challenge for educational institutions too. The range of skills demanded of land managers can be seen in published statements concerning this activity:

Aspects on Education and Training 27

Management is concerned with what happens between the main decision-making structure and the performance of the operational task (Stapleton, 1994).

Management is defined as the selection of goals and the planning, procurement, organisation, co-ordination and control of the necessary resources (land) for their achievement. Management is concerned with the dynamics of circumstance and activity and is generally motivated by the need to economise in the use of resources and time in achieving predetermined objectives (cit. Allsopp in Stapleton, 1994).

Land Administration is the process of determining, recording, and disseminating information about the ownership, value, and use of land in order to implement land management policies. Land management encompasses all those activities associated with the management of land as a resource that are required to achieve sustainable development (Dale, 2000).

The fundamental principle of land management is sustainability, the combination of production with conservation (Young, 1998).

But what is the job description of a land manager? Firstly, the land manager is an administrator of land. He/she has to register the ownership of land, to record the size and the boundaries of parcels, and finally to evaluate the land. But the land manager also is a co-ordinator of land specific tasks. In this role, he/she:

- has to control or be aware of the many factors that concern the land;
- is responsible for the collection of geometric, topologic, and thematic data of land;
- is responsible for the maintenance of the data and, through using that data and knowledge;
- is able to inform the public about land.

It has also been proposed that land managers also become mediators of existing problems between people and the land, such as these problems identified in the Bathurst Declaration by the International Federation of Surveyors (FIG), and by the United Nations (FIG, 1999) such as the:

- degradation of land due to unsustainable land use practices;
- lack of land for suitable urban development;
- lack of security of tenure;
- increasing vulnerability to disaster;
- destruction of bio-diversity;
- lack of adequate planning and of effective land administration; and
- tensions between environmental conservation and development.

Finally, the land manager has to advise customers on all requests of land. The job description of the land manager can be summarised in short as the real power behind decision-makers (UEL, 1998). However, decision-makers themselves are land managers, although at a policy level. They have to decide

28 *Methodologies, Models and Instruments*

on the objectives of land use and on available resources. Strategies must be developed and administrative structures have to be implemented to achieve the defined goals. These tasks will be handled on a management level, although all measures to meet the proposed strategies will be realised on a third level - the operational level (adapted to Steudler and Williamson, 2002).

The widespread field of activities is reflected in the following list of required skills for the profession of land managers:

- political understanding;
- ethnologic awareness;
- economic knowledge;
- administrative knowledge;
- social competence;
- natural understanding;
- technical knowledge;
- languages;
- dynaxity (dynamic and flexibility).

Depending upon the responsibilities in land management (political, administrative, or operational) the required quantity of knowledge in each of the outlined skills will vary. The inter-relationship between skills and responsibilities is exemplified in Figure 4.2.

In general, educational and training courses disregard the different required job profiles of land managers. The programmes are mainly targeted at the operational level in profession. Experts working on the political and administrative level of profession acquire the additionally-needed knowledge and skills for the other two levels in a postgraduate education or in a 'learning by doing' process.

Whilst it possible to identify the skills required for land management, it far less easy to define the responsibility for the education and training of land managers, and defining the importance of that education and training within the field of land management.

Education and training

Information on the surveying institutions around the world is available in the Surveying Education Data Base (EBS) of the International Federation of Surveyors (FIG). Over four hundred courses are documented in the database, categorised by the field of specialisation and qualification (Table 4.1). Of course, the number of registered courses in the EDB is not complete, but the distribution of courses provided worldwide can be estimated on the basis of this data.

To obtain feedback about the relevance of education and training in the different fields of surveying activities, the authors analysed the results of an Internet-Search-Engine.

Aspects on Education and Training 29

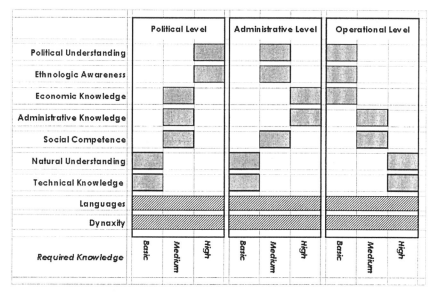

Figure 4.2 Job specifications of land managers in different levels of responsibility

Table 4.1 Distribution of provided courses in surveying dependent on the field of specialisation

Field of Specialisation	Number of Courses	% of all Courses
Geodetic, Land and Cadastral and/or Engineering Surveying	193	25.6
Planning, Development and Land Use Management	152	20.2
Building/Architectural Surveying	51	6.8
Hydrographic Surveying	41	5.4
Minerals Surveying	24	3.2
Property	78	10.4
Quantity	57	7.5
Construction Economics	52	6.9
Valuation and Real Estate Management	76	10.1
Geographic Information Management/Systems	29	3.9
SUM	*753*	*100.0*

Source: FIG Education Database (http://www.fig.net/figtree/indexmain.htm), March 2003.

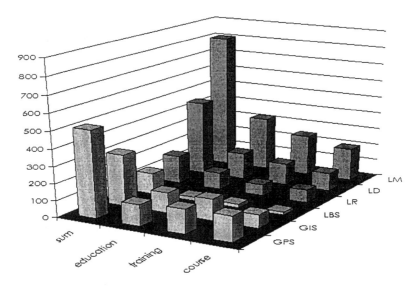

Figure 4.3 Results of Web-Search (in thousands of findings) dependent on keywords (GPS...Global Positioning System, GIS...Geographic Information Systems, LBS...Location Based Services, LR...Land Reform, LD...Land Development, LM...Land Management) **and filters** (education, training, and course)
Source: 'All-the-web'-Search Engine, March 2003.

The investigation was started with the search for keywords relevant in the education of surveyors. The Search Engine found approximately 500,000 websites including the exact phrase 'Global Positioning System' in the text and approximately 800,000 web pages containing the exact term 'Land Management'. This search for each keyword was repeated using additional word filters. The detailed results of the various queries can be seen in Figure 4.3. Thus, using the keyword 'Land Management' and the word filter 'Education' 322,000 web sites were listed.

The total number of web sites found related to a keyword will not be discussed in this paper. The outlined sums are not significant to the numbers of employed persons within a branch of surveying. The queries only should outline the relevance of education and training in the field of 'land management' (land reform, land development) and in the field of 'modern surveying techniques'. In general, the importance of educational and training aspects is very high in the surveying profession. Forty percent of all websites found with the topics 'Land Management' and 'Geographic Information Systems' also include the word 'education'. Furthermore, in 'Land Reform' a specific demand on training and education can be derived from the result that 60 of 100 websites found also contained 'education'. Similar results were obtained using 'training' and 'course' as word filters.

Aspects on Education and Training 31

Boundary conditions in education and training

Science was and is never independent from the spirit of age (Weizäcker, 1997).

The spirit of age also significantly influenced rigorous education and training, especially in industrialised countries. Until the early-1980s, higher education in land management was focused principally on technical methods and technical tools. More recently, the field of profession and education expanded to economical issues and when during the 1990s many international conventions and declarations started to claim 'sustainable development of land', society also began to change their basic values with a consequence that political, scientific, and educational programmes in land management were expanded to include environmental and ecological components. Currently, unemployment, the rigorous decrease of agricultural enterprises, and the migration to cities require the integration of social elements into the management of land. Furthermore, this trend from technique-orientated specialists to multifunction-educated experts can also be observed in developing countries - with a time shift of some years. Thus, the initial boundary condition in education is the spirit of age: curricula developments are driven - consciously or unconsciously - by the spirit of age.

New techniques in the field of data collection and data processing have also shaped the education in land management within the last years. New surveying and data processing methods have been developed, which two decades ago were unknown by most surveyors. These include:

- Global Positioning Systems (GPS);
- Geographic Information Systems (GIS);
- Laser Scanning;
- Location Based Services (LBS);
- High resolution digital image data; and
- Semi-automatic and automatic image processing.

During this period, the use of new technologies led on one hand to an increasing effectiveness of data acquisition and on the other to an improvement in data quality. The need of huge sets of geodata could be satisfied by automatic procedures for data acquisition. Object detection led to additional research activities in the surveying industry, and the first results to recognise and classify objects out of digital images were achieved in photogrammetry and remote sensing. This period coincided with the launch of generations of new instruments and new technologies, which in turn generates a permanent level of re-adaptation of the contents of educational programmes.

The second boundary condition is that the rapid development of new surveying technologies has created another issue of education: that of life-long learning. In the past, the theoretical knowledge once acquired provided a good basis, sufficient for most tasks in the profession of surveying and for working with specific instruments. Of course, the technical skills for working with the new technology had to be updated - but this could be achieved in short-term training programmes. Nowadays the recently developed instruments and techniques also demand additional basic theory. Universities and educational institutions should, in co-operation with the professional practice, offer the possibility for life-long upgrading of the theoretical framework for land managers.

Another boundary condition is the trend to harmonise education. In academic education, the countrywide standardisation was defined by the national legal framework and/or the national authorities. With increasing worldwide mobility of students (move and study) and that of professional experts, the requirements of harmonisation are extended to a global level. The efforts to achieve a standardised education system in the European Union are an important step in this direction. Commission 2 of the International Federation of Surveyors has initiated many activities to enable an international mutual recognition of professional qualifications and quality assurance in surveying education (FIG, 1999a; FIG, 2002; Enemark and Prendergast, 2001).

The global competition of universities and educational institutions too has an important impact on the educational systems, enhanced also by the increasing mobility of students. At many universities, the number of students is a main factor for receiving money. Due to the trend of reducing public financing for educational institutions (especially in the EU) the competition between the institutions in recruiting students will increase over the next few years.

Some open questions in education

Lecturers are often involved in the development of curricula. As mentioned above, the reasons for the ongoing maintenance of educational and training programmes are a combination of the progress in technical development, the changing economic and political situation, modified legal frameworks, and the shifting concept of society. In general, the curricular can be fitted in a perfect manner regarding the exterior boundary conditions but the authors recognised also some unanswered questions in the training and educational programs of land managers.

Who should teach land management? Land managers are expected to cover a wide spectrum of knowledge as outlined in the first part of this chapter. In the past the knowledge for land managers was offered and provided for in the academic programmes of surveying education. However, with the changing demands upon land managers, the purely technical contents of curricula were extended with economic, ecological, social, and legal issues. Of course, the teaching of the new subjects lay in the responsibility of experts in the specific profession, but under the umbrella of a course of surveying study. Is this also necessary in the future?

Are the academic staff educators or trainers? The dilemma is well known. Universities want to educate the students and the students themselves want training to fulfil the demands of the labour market. From this arises a conflict between theoretical education and practical training. The problem lies not in universities having to work practically using specific software or specific instruments but in the time available for education. Both laboratory work and fieldwork are very time-consuming educational modules. In general, the statement of the German photogrammetrist Otto von Gruber is also valid in the field of land management, 'Nothing is more practical than a good theory'. Project-organised education could be a method to solve this Gordean knot.

Is there a difference in teaching land management or international land management? Land Management always depends on political, legal, social, and economic frame conditions of a specific country. From this point of view the education programmes must differ between different countries. In reality, the curricula are similar all over the world with the trend of standardisation. The specific skills and knowledge needed for international land management must be acquired in additional courses.

Should universities educate researchers or engineers? Researchers have to discover knowledge (it must be new, additional to available knowledge), engineers have to design systems based on rules (a good solution, which had been used in the past is still a good solution). Modern educational systems allow the choice between both branches of profession.

Should the virtual academy become reality in the education of land managers? eLearning, virtual education, long distance learning, and guided-self learning are tools and methods that may be used to support knowledge transfer and to enable virtual lecture rooms. Will they change the whole educational systems? Can they substitute traditional lecturing or replace the teachers? These are questions that cannot yet be answered since the access to electronic media is the limiting factor for this new technology mow. In 2000, only 20% of the population had access to the Internet. Fifty percent of the population of North America was able to surf in the Internet whereas only approximately 5% used the Internet all over the world. However, there is no doubt that eLearning brings about new opportunities for knowledge transfer - also in terms of life-long learning.

Summary and outlook

This chapter has outlined some aspects of education in the field of land management. The authors could only give a short overview of the required skills and knowledge for the profession of land managers. Finally, the open questions and new challenges in the academic education in general, and for land managers in particular, were presented.

In future, the rapid evolution of surveying and teaching technology and globalisation will shape education in land management. The intention is not to harmonise curricula but to balance the need for standardisation with the flexibility of altering the educational programmes adapted to the demands of a dynamic

34 *Methodologies, Models and Instruments*

world. Educators, trainers, and international institutions should consider these challenges.

References

Creuzer, P., 2000. *Support of Good Land Administration by the Work of the UNECE Working Party on Land Administration*. Zeitschrift für Vermessungswesen. 125.Jahrgang, Heft 10/2000, 349-352, Konrad Wittwer Verlag, Stuttgart.

Dale, P., 2000. *Surveying Engineering and Global Land Management*, Zeitschrift für Vermessungswesen. 125.Jahrgang, Heft 5/2000, 147-154, Konrad Wittwer Verlag, Stuttgart.

Enemark, S. and Prendergast, P., (eds.), 2001. *Enhancing Professional Competence of Surveyors in Europe*, A joint CLGE (Council of European Geodetic Surveyors) and FIG (International Federation of Surveyors) Report, Copenhagen, Denmark.

FIG, 1996. *Continuing Professional Development*, FIG-Publication Nr. 15, The International Federation of Surveyors (FIG), Frederiksberg, Denmark.

FIG, 1999. *The Bathurst Declaration on Land Administration for Sustainable Development*, FIG-Publication Nr. 21, Copenhagen, Denmark.

FIG, 1999a. *Quality Assurance in Surveying Education*, FIG-Publication, Copenhagen, Denmark.

FIG, 2002. *Mutual Recognition of Professional Qualifications*. FIG-Publication Nr. 27, Copenhagen, Denmark.

Hartermann, W., 1999. *Der 'Geodät 2000' – Realität und Vision an der Schwelle zum 21.Jahrhundert*, Zeitschrift für Vermessungswesen, 124.Jahrgang, Heft 2/1999, 42-45, Verlag Konrad Wittwer GmbH, Stuttgart 1.

MADAME, 2000. *Methods for Access to Data and Metadata in Europe*, Practitioner's Forum on Institutional and Organisational Issues in Increasing Access to Public Sector Information.

Magel, H., 2000. *Nachhaltige Entwicklung - zur globalen Verantwortung von Bodenordnung und Landentwicklung*. In: Weber, G. (Hrsg.) Zukunftsperspektiven von Raumplanung und Ländlicher Neuordnung.

Stapleton, T., 1994. *Estate Management Practice*, Estate Gazette, A Reed Business Publication, The Estates Gazette Limited, London.

Steudler, D. and Williamson, I.P., 2002. A framework for benchmarking land administration systems, *Proceedings of FIG XXII International Congress*, Washington DC.

UeL, 1997. *Geographical and Land Information Management. BSc Honours Programme*, Leaflet for Courses, School of Surveying, University of East London.

Weizäcker, e.U.v., 1997. *Globale Wissenschaft - globale Wirtschaft - globale Umwelt*. In: Die BOKU, Heft 2, 17-24, Herausgeber: Universität für Bodenkultur.

Young, A., 1998. *Land Resources - Now and for the Future*, Cambridge University Press, Cambridge.

Chapter 5

Land Fragmentation in Central Europe: How and Whether to use Western Experience

Terry van Dijk

Introduction

The Iron Curtain that separated the Eastern Block from Western Europe fell around 1990. This event changed the name of the region containing the former socialist countries. The countries closest to Western Europe, i.e. Poland, Hungary, the Czech Republic, Slovakia, and Slovenia are now referred to as Central European Countries (CECs). The reference is mainly used in combination with the adjacent region of Eastern European countries, Central and Eastern European Countries (CEECs), to which Romania and Bulgaria belong. The division between Central and Eastern Europe is subject to debate (Dingsdale, 1999).

Although the development paths of the individual states diverge (Lerman, 2001; Davidova and Buckwell, 2000), extensive rural areas in Central Europe suffer from extreme fragmentation of land ownership. Land consolidation, an instrument that has been widely applied in Western Europe, is expected to be a way of dealing with land fragmentation. However, specific regional conditions have to be considered in order to make land consolidation successful in Central Europe. The important question is how to determine what differences matter?

The emergence of Central European fragmentation

In the Central European region, land has had a special political position throughout the last 60 years. This history is the key to understanding the status quo, as well as the driving forces.

During socialist times, there was a constant effort to accumulate land into public use and, if possible, public ownership. The ideology regarded land as an endowment of society and private ownership was the expropriation of public wealth for private gain (Dawson, 1984). The socialist ideal was the establishment of large production units in which every member contributed his of her share and society as a whole would benefit from its yield.

The exact implications of socialist perspectives towards land are subject to widespread misperceptions. In contradiction to what is widely believed, certainly not all private property was erased after 1945 (Brooks, 1993). Many families retained title to land and some never lost ownership, even though their land was collectively managed. The proportion of land owned by the state in state-farms in Central Europe was never greater than 25%. In Poland, collectivisation failed completely. Thus, the concept of private property, unlike that of the former Soviet Union states (Dekker, 2001) did not disappear. Creed (1992) even describes systems of allowing private activities within the co-operatives in Bulgaria, a country considered to have been very strict in applying the Soviet model of collective agriculture. Furthermore, collective agriculture was not uniform throughout the region, and was not a failure in all cases (see Meurs, 1999; and Pryor, 1992).

Despite the variations in the applications of socialism, in all cases a retarded ownership structure was preserved by the political climate. The remainder of private property was generally prevented from expanding and developing, as was clearly the case in Poland (Borek, 1993), whilst collective farming froze the underlying ownership structure for several decades.

The events of the early 1990s resulted in the restoration of this small-scale structure and the transformation into a market economy through breaking up collective structures into private property. Time consuming and complicated privatisation processes were executed, of which Swinnen (1996) gives an overview and explanations. In all cases where, despite collective land use, original ownership titles were still in place, the governments had no other choice than reinstating this property. In those cases where ownership titles had been seized, attempts were made to restitute the original property.

Although this was sensible from the point of view of historical justice, the result has been devastating. Ownership is on an extremely small scale, partly because some of the original owners already had passed away and the restituted parcels were divided among the heirs. Also, many parcels fell in hands of people who were neither willing nor capable of using the land. Furthermore, the facilities in rural areas were not always suitable for private farming. Co-operative assets like machines and buildings became useless, and vast areas of land have fallen fallow.

Severity of fragmentation

For an analysis of the severity of Central European fragmentation, it is important not to mix up land ownership and land use problems. Land ownership fragmentation is severe in all Central European countries but land use could be much better. For example, land users (i.e. farmers) could rent several ownership parcels and use them as one production unit. Because the disadvantages of fragmentation are most strongly experienced by land users (in terms of production inefficiency), the use structure is most interesting here.

It is hard to make a clear and exact comparison between the Central European countries because statistical definitions vary and many legal forms exist. Tillack and

Schulze (2000); and Swinnen *et al* (1997) are collections of papers by experts from the region that give a kaleidoscopic overview of both land ownership and land use fragmentation. Table 5.1 is an attempt to present the statistical material in a way that makes comparison possible.

Table 5.1   Impression of land use fragmentation midway the 1990s (TAL=total agricultural land)

		Number	Share of TAL	Average size (ha)	Remarks
Poland	Private farms	2,100,000	76.4	6.3	50% under 5 ha
(Borek, 1993)	State farms	1,300	18.0	2.7	
Hungary	Private farms	1,400,000	17.0	0.8	44% under 5 ha
(Harcsa et al,	State farms	136	15.0	7.0	
1998)	Co-operations	1,267	68.0	3.5	
Bulgaria	Private farms	1,777,000	52.5	1.5	86% under 1 ha
(Davidova et	State farms	980	6.5	311.0	
al, 1997)	Co-operations	2,344	40.8	815.3	
	Farming companies	122	0.7	283.5	
Romania	Private farms	3,973,000	52.1	1.9	40% under 1 ha
(Benedek,	Private companies	3,800	11.6	443.0	
2000)	Family associations	9,500	6.8	105.0	
	State farms	560	11.8	3.1	
Czech	Natural entities	24,380	23.8	34.6	
Republic	State farms	41	1.7	732.0	
(Voltr, 2000)	Legal entities	2,753	74.6	966.0	
Slovakia	Private sector	8,632	79.2	201.0	54% under 5 ha
(Kabat and	Public sector	299	20.8	1,526.0	
Hagedorn,					
1997)					

One commonality in the region is that the land use structure is bimodal. This means that there is a very large group of very small land users and a small group of very large land users. The middle-sized farms, that are so characteristic to Western European family farming, tend to fail. Thus, in land use statistics, fragmentation is most serious when the percentage of farms smaller than 5 ha are considered. However, the proportion of agricultural land occupied by farms under 5 ha is relatively small and hence the problem seems less serious.

The balance between the small-scale land users and the larger production units differs throughout the region. Slovakia and the Czech Republic have the best land use structure, with some three-quarters of all agricultural land used in large units (Voltr,

38   *Methodologies, Models and Instruments*

2000; Kabat and Hagedorn, 1997). In contrast, Romania and Bulgaria are very fragmented, with more than half of all agricultural land being used in units smaller than 2 ha, corresponding to 4 and 1.8 million farmers respectively (Davidova *et al*, 1997; Benedek, 2000). Hungary's characteristics are intermediate (Harcsa *et al*, 1998).

What makes fragmentation a problem

The leads naturally to three important questions, namely why fragmentation is a problem, under what circumstances and to whom? However, it should be noted that fragmentation might be an advantage since it reduces the risk of an entire crop being destroyed by flooding, diseases, or hailstorms.

In terms of separation of ownership and use, the negative effects of fragmentation mainly come from the lack of investments in land. Investments in infrastructure such as, irrigation or soil improvement must be paid back over long periods of time, and tenancy generally gives too little security to allow such expenditures. Moreover, the essential loans for making investments in the first place cannot be obtained without suitable collateral. Thus, without investment productivity will fall below its optimal level.

The disadvantage of a low average farm size is also clear. The amount of cultivated land just does not produce enough to earn a living. In certain regions, off-farm income can supplement the revenues from the farm, thus overcoming the farm-size restriction (for instance in the Italian small farms). Regardless of the limited farm production, each farm-unit is physically separated from others by fences, ditches or hedgerows, and these elements, together with infrastructure, amount to a loss of productive land, which is much higher than in large-scale landscapes. Small farms negatively affect productive acreage and the land/man-ratio.

This land loss also relates to internal farm fragmentation. The total length of parcel borders increases with fragmentation. Apart from the land loss by separating elements, parcel borders generally receive less fertiliser and pesticides, and they are more susceptible to wind damage and drought. When parcels are far apart, the time and fuel involved in travelling is another disadvantage. Parcels located at greater distance from the production unit are generally cultivated less intensively. Internal fragmentation negatively affects productive acreage and efficiency.

The economical implications of fragmentation are loss of production and time and, through these, farmers' income as well. However, not every economically sub-optimal situation is a problem. In post-war programmes from Western governments (for instance Hofstee, 1956), the essential argument for intervention is parity between urban and rural standards of living. If (i) the standard of living in cities in considerably higher than in rural areas, (ii) rural residents are aware of this difference, and (iii) land fragmentation is believed to contribute to this difference, then fragmentation is a problem to farmers and regions.

This problem-definition implies that no fixed figures are at hand with which a region can be assessed on its fragmentation. We cannot derive that a farm is not viable below 4.2 ha. The parity issue is a matter of balance. A booming industry and service sector in the major cities (such as may be currently witnessed in Warsaw) demand large farms to reach a comparable standard of living for rural dwellers. Thus, the threshold for the fragmentation problem depends on the prosperity in cities. In addition, many other factors than land fragmentation alone determine the farmers' income (see Hughes, 2000 for case studies). For example, on a 4 ha, 10-parcel farm, the income can be acceptable when high prices are paid for the produce, inputs are cheap and marketing channels suit small-scale farming. Under conditions of a 'price scissors' and unsuitable marketing, however, that same farm could be far from viable.

The disadvantages of fragmentation, food production, and rural incomes, have varying impacts on the various administrative levels. On a regional level, considerations of income can be an important reason to ask for support from the national government. The national government will be susceptible for parity in income and for national food security and agricultural exports. Food security is not a problem in Central Europe, but export of agricultural produce can be of national importance. In Bulgaria and Romania, for example, the favourable natural endowments (warm climate, fertile soil) are the main economic asset that as such must be exploited. The presence of major non-agricultural assets could have eased the urgency of fragmentation. At another level, the European Union neither wants additional agricultural surpluses nor rural poverty. This paradox will remain a heavily debated complication to the current accession process. At a global level, in the light of a growing world population, all loss of production may be regarded as a problem, but fragmentation is only a minor impediment to world food production.

Land consolidation: differences explained

For the purpose of this chapter, a comparison is made of land consolidation in Germany and the Netherlands. In order to make this more relevant, a specific time-period has been chosen, the 1954 Land Consolidation Acts of Germany and the Netherlands, respectively, since in the formulation of these laws, the mechanism of parcel-exchange could be observed more clearly than in later versions. In the more recent developments of those Acts, the parcel-exchange mechanism did not change, with the most recent developments being focussed upon speeding up the process and cost-effectiveness.

The official aim of land consolidation, as defined in by the law, is slightly broader in Germany than in the Netherlands. The 1954 Dutch Law on Land Consolidation indicates that:

> Land consolidation is executed based on an agreement or on the law in the interest of agriculture, horticulture, forestry, or cattle breeding (§2).

> A land-consolidation agreement is an agreement in which three or more owners commit themselves to merge certain real estate they own, reallocate the resulting landmass and distribute the ownership among each other in a notary act (§4, line 1).

40 *Methodologies, Models and Instruments*

The German Law on Land Consolidation from the same period defined land consolidation as follows (Steuer, 1956):

> In the interest of agriculture, forestry as well as general rural quality, fragmented or inefficiently shaped rural land ownership can be consolidated - considering aspects of farm management - or improved in other ways (§1).

The Dutch and German Land Consolidation Laws from 1954 were compared, giving a complete overview of the discrepancies. For the goal of this article, not every difference is equally important or interesting. Minor differences can be a case of coincidence and very hard to explain. The larger and more profound differences do matter. Here we seek for explanations for the differences that are listed in Table 5.2 (Dutch and German paragraphs respectively).

Table 5.2   Comparison between Dutch and German land consolidation laws

Condition	Dutch Paragraphs	German Paragraphs
Provisions regarding tenancy	§18-§27; §28	§70; §71
Decision to proceed	§37-§54	§4; §5
Valuation procedure	§55-§78	§27-§36
Title purification	§5	*no match*
Body of participants	*no match*	§16-§26; §151-§153

The major differences that will be addressed in this section justify the assumption that they are not coincidental. Both the Netherlands and Germany were and are democratic countries with an important agricultural lobby in politics. Thus, provisions that would have unsuitable and damaging for agriculture would have been criticised, while provisions that were regarded as desirable probably would have been introduced. Therefore, over time the Land Consolidation Law would be the optimal fit between the agriculture subject and that law, and it would be naturally expected that differences in land consolidation procedures can be explained by underlying factors.

Provisions regarding tenancy

According to German Law, tenants of farmland cannot claim an efficient land reallocation through land consolidation. This led to the assumption that tenancy was considered to be unimportant in Germany and, in fact, in 1949 only 5% of all agricultural land was rented. In contrast, the share of tenancy in the Netherlands in that period was about 56%. The tenancy factor in Germany is aggravated by the fact that tenancy was especially important among the smaller farms (those with an area of less than 5 ha), whilst most farms larger 10 hectares were owner-occupied. Thus, small farmers are likely to have had little influence on tenancy policies.

However, after World War II the importance of tenancy grew rapidly. By 1971, the average share of tenancy rose to 16.4%, whilst the size of the farms that rented significant amounts of land increased (Table 5.2). Whereas in 1950, farms larger than 50 hectares only rented 3% of their land, this had increased to between twenty and thirty percent by 1971. However, despite the increased importance of tenancy, the regulations were not altered when the Act was revised in 1976.

A better explanation might be that Dutch tenancy needed more protection because of its different nature. Dutch tenants enjoy increasing protection. In 1941 regulations were adopted for the price of tenancy and the owner of tenancy land had to respect a minimum term for tenancy agreements. Later, tenancy rights could be continued in the family, and the tenant was entitled to pre-emption right (being the first to buy the rented land when it is for sale).

Table 5.3   Percentage of the tenancy land in Bavaria, farmed within each farm-size class, given for three points in time

	Size of holding (ha)								
	0.5-2	2-5	5-10	10-20	20-30	30-50	50-100	>100	Average
1949	20.6	15.5	9.4	5.4	2.6	2.2	3.6	2.5	5.3
1960	12.9	14.7	13.1	10.3	5.4	3.9	5.1	1.5	7.1
1971	12.4		15.1	16.8	16.2	15.7	22.8	32.9	16.4

Source: Bavarian Statistical Office, various years.

In contrast, the German tenant was scarcely protected by a Tenancy Act: in fact, here was no Tenancy Act. Even today, only the Civil Law has some provisions on tenancy, but neither prescribes minimum terms nor regulations in case an owner decides to withdraw its land from a tenancy market. In practice, the low level of protection of tenants caused tenancy agreements to be valid for only a short period (one or several years) and often without any written contract.

Decision to proceed

On first sight, one might get the impression that the Dutch procedure protects the interests of farmers better than the German procedure. Before a Dutch land consolidation project is started, a request must be filed, followed by a long procedure involving a national Land Consolidation Commission and the provincial parliament. Subsequently, the participants have to vote on whether or not they are interested. The German Law merely notes that the authorities can decide to initiate a land consolidation project.

Historic developments give some indication of the origin of this situation. In the case of the Bavarian procedure, which had a significant influence on the content of the Federal Law, the procedure did not differ greatly from the Netherlands. There was a similar voting system but over time, the demands for a favourable outcome of the voting became less rigorous. It was, therefore, a logical step to abolish voting in 1954. However, why was the power of the farmers to stop land consolidation gradually eroded?

With the decline of the power of farmers in the decision-process of consolidate, there was an opposite development in their power later during the process. The 1886 Law provided a land consolidation authority with complete executive responsibilities in the process. In 1922, however, a Body of Participants was introduced. This meant that the participants received control over the process. Obviously, this was a success, because the Federal Law adopted the same principle (top-down initiation, bottom-up execution). Thus, whilst the decision making process might appear authoritarian, the top-down approach is compensated by the subsequent influence of the Body of Participants. In other words, because the rest of the process is so democratic, it would not make sense for an authority to initiate land consolidation without anyone interested in it.

Valuation procedure

Should every parcel within the land consolidation area have the same quality, reallocation could take place on the basis of area, with every farmer receiving the same acreage as he contributed. However, when 5 ha of well-drained soil are replaced by 5 ha of very wet soil, the farmer is likely to protest. This is why valuation is so important.

In both cases, valuation is on a relative scale and the actual market value is not actually determined. It is more important to know that one type of soil is more productive and, thus, categories of value are made. In the Netherlands as well as in Germany, for every project a unique set of categories is determined.

An important difference is the composition of the valuation commission. According to the Federal German Law, the valuation commission consists of agricultural experts. However, the Board of the Body of Participants must be present to advise the experts on region-specific details although it can be ignored. In the Netherlands, the valuation commission consists of farmers, preferably from the project area. They are trained in objectively valuing the land of other participants.

One would expect that in Germany there are more factors that are important but not necessarily related to the soil. The relief of Germany is more varied than in the Netherlands, and there are microclimates within valleys. The microclimates can cause specific sites to be subject to regular hailstorms or late frosts. Experts who are unfamiliar with the area might be unaware of these factors. The Board must inform them of these details. In the Netherlands, factors that cannot be derived from soil characteristics seem much less important than in Germany. It is possible that the German legislation has been more perceptive to the disadvantage of valuation by locals, who might look after their own interests, whereas experts from outside the area should be more impartial. Conversely, the expert report has to be approved by all participants.

Both Dutch and German legislation use the production potential as a value for reallocation, although the Dutch procedure takes into consideration the contextual factors. However, this 'broad value' is not used for the reallocation, but for determining the share of the total costs to the participants.

Title purification

The Dutch land consolidation projects are concluded by adoption of all new owners' rights into the land registry. Only then is the newly established allocation legal and official. The German practice is identical. However, Dutch Law specifically states that the newly established situation is definite. Normally, proper legal evidence can lead to rights that have been in place for years being reconsidered. For example, Mr. Green has bought land from Mr. Brown nine years ago, and has used it since. When a Mr. Miller can prove that at that time Mr. Brown had falsely presented himself as the owner and Miller in fact was the owner, the ownership of Mr. Green can be drawn into question. Currently, the Dutch land registry is considered almost as reliable as a title registration, but in the heydays of land consolidation, the above-mentioned insecurity could not be ignored.

According to the Dutch §5, no reconsideration is possible after the new rights have been allocated and established in the land registry. Naturally, before this title purification takes place there will have been a very accurate check and appeal procedure to ensure that no rights are lost in this action.

The advantage of this title purification is significant. A notary normally would have to check whether or not a selling party indeed is the rightful owner. This check might involve extensive research into the history of the real estate involved. Title purification means that research before the time of purification is not necessary any more. This way, the land registry becomes more reliable; the chance that a transaction will prove not valid becomes smaller.

So why don't the Germans use this mechanism? The advantages are clear and the effort is relatively small. The explanation is that they do not use it because they do not need it, since their land registry is basically different from the Dutch land registry. In the Netherlands, transactions are recorded (deeds registration). If a transaction is legal, the buyer is by definition the new rightful owner of the real estate. As explained above, this holds a certain degree of uncertainty for the right holder, because in exceptional cases it might turn out that the transaction was not fully legal. Title purification mitigates this uncertainty.

In the German 'Grundbuch', the owner of each real estate object is recorded (title registration) which means that the right holder is the owner by law. A transaction will change the owner in the register, potentially causing similar reliability problems as in the Netherlands. However, in the Grundbuch-system the mutations (i.e. transactions) are checked so thoroughly that the accuracy is beyond any doubt.[1]

The reliability of German land registry is further underlined by §30, line 2 that states that the old situation, as recorded in the land registry, is considered beyond any doubt and is therefore not surveyed. In the Netherlands, it is surveyed, updating the existing cadastral information.

---

[1] With proper and accurate information-management, a deeds registration can render it virtually indistinguishable from title registries, as is the case in the Netherlands right now. See Zevenbergen (2002) for more detailed information on land registry systems.

Body of Participants

From the Law, it would appear that the Dutch participants do not have much influence during the project. After voting in favour or against the land consolidation project, they seem to be left waiting and hoping for a favourable ending.

In practice, however, the participants have more influence than the Law suggests, notably a very important extra-legal stage in the process that is effectively a wish-session. On this session, every participant has a personal conversation with the local Committee during which they can express their thoughts concerning the parcelling problems of the area in general, and their farm in particular. Furthermore, participants can deposit up to three alternative changes in their personal parcelling. These alternatives are recorded in writing and serve as a basis for the design of the reallocation plan. The alternatives can also include the wish to preserve the original parcelling, although no guarantees can be made.

Although the wish-session softens the seemingly extreme autonomy the local Committee has following the voting, the Bavarian procedure is still much more participatory with those involved remaining in control over the proceedings throughout the project. The history of the Body of Participants goes back to the Bavarian Land Consolidation revision of 1922. At that point the Body of Participants was introduced (Genossenschaftprinzip). Thus, every land consolidation project in Bavaria has started with all participants merging into a body of public right. In 1954 the Federal German Law also adopted this principle, and still continues it.

The Body elects a Board from within, which has far reaching authority within the project. It takes decisions concerning public facilities and cost distribution among the participants. In Bavaria the responsibilities are even more extensive, comprising the design of the reallocation plan, valuation of land and reservation of land for public facilities (Bisle, 1986). During the process, the Board is chaired by a land consolidation official. He contributes legal knowledge and agricultural expertise. In addition, he has a decisive vote when the Board is indecisive.

The reason for the emergence of the Body of Participants must be sought in the emancipation of the citizens throughout the German society (Schlosser, personal comment). World War II marked the end of the Bavarian monarchy that had disregarded the interests of civilians for so long. The counter effect right after the fall of the Wittenbacher-monarchy was a strong call for civilian-participation in the governmental process in many different facets of everyday life. The Body of Participants has proved to be a very effective element in the German procedure. All participants feel responsible and involved in the process.

Today, this principle still maintained. The main idea is 'not against but in co-operation with the farmers' (Nicht gegen sondern mit den Bauern). In the Netherlands, a similar movement has started in the 1980s (Van Lier, 2000), when the top-down approach encountered increasing resistance.

Conclusion

This latter part of this chapter has sought to explain the differences that were discovered as a result of the comparison. Most paragraphs from the Laws have a counterpart in the other country. In addition, there are paragraphs that are unique for the respective countries, some of which are coincidental. For instance, the importance of local knowledge in the valuation commission does not have a clear correlation with the diversity in growing conditions, assuming that factors that are not related to soil type are more important in case of hilly topography.

For four differences, a plausible explanation was found. The explanations would have been more certain and more generally applicable in case of a larger set of countries. Even then, mathematical regression analysis in order to postulate general patterns is not permitted between cases (Yin, 1994). Generalisation of case study results should be done through so-called analytic generalisation. In that instance, you generalise to theoretical proposition and not to populations or universes. It seems reasonable to assume that there can be various reasons for differences between countries.

The status of tenants in a project depends on the level of tenancy-protection. In the Dutch case, tenants had a very firm claim on the land they used, which caused land consolidation to reallocate land use in an efficient way, and not only land ownership. But since Hungarian and Bulgarian tenants are relatively weak, in a legal-technical sense, it does not seem sensible to consider their interests in reassigning parcels. If bureaucracy and transaction-taxing is not too restricting, tenancy can rearrange itself after ownership has been rearranged, such as in Bavarian projects. This goes for all rights to land that allow simple informal rearranging.

The desirability of title purification depends on how reliable the land registry is. Central European land registries typically are in the process of being established and privatisation matters do not have a positive effect on the accuracy. Title purification may be a way to give landowners more security on the possession of their land and may eventually increase the quality of the rural land registry as a whole.

The origin of the Body of Participants-concept can be traced down a public need for civilians' participation. If we relate this to the Central Europeans' scepticism toward government interference, it seems very sensible to apply this type of democratic project-management. It furthermore enables top-down initiation of projects, which allows the government to set priorities on which regions optimisation of agricultural production can take place and which regions are to be preserved because of their scenic or environmental qualities.

The settlement pattern determines the usefulness of village-renewal and farm-reallocation. The Dutch landscape is dominated by separate farmsteads scattered across the landscape. Farm-reallocation was widely practised here in order to achieve a more balanced dispersion of farms. In the clustered settlement pattern of Bavaria, farm-reallocation was useful for villages that were too congested with farming activity for acceptable working and living conditions, but the expected disruption of social structures prevented its excessive use. Farmers' villages remained to be the standard, and therefore village-renewal emerged. Since the Hungarian and Bulgarian overall rural settlement structure is clustered, village renewal is a logical choice.

46 *Methodologies, Models and Instruments*

Finally is suggested that countries such as Hungary and Bulgaria should choose an ownership consolidation based on the Body of Participants-concept, which concentrates on improving conditions for farming, leads to title purification and is supported by village-renewal.

Remarks

The methodology presented here facilitates institutional transplantation. Through these steps, one can modify for instance land consolidation, thus achieving a better fit with local conditions in the recipient country.

It is essential to bear in mind, however, that before adjusting the instrument to local conditions it has to be clear whether the instrument is applicable at all in the donor country. Namely, it could very well be that the similarity in problems that led to the suggestion for transplantation, in reality shows crucial differences.

In the Bulgarian case, for instance, the fragmentation figures for both land ownership and for land use are bad. The connection to land consolidation seems obvious. Nonetheless, at least two fundamental differences suggest that land consolidation is not applicable at all, not even when it is modified to fit local conditions.

One difference is hidden under the double meaning of fragmentation. The word 'fragmentation' refers to the division of one farm into too many parcels, but also to the average farm size in a region. Western European land consolidation mainly dealt with the first type, while the second definition applies to Bulgaria.

A second major difference is the type of landowners. In Western Europe the land users always have been personally committed to their land, and by and large were prepared to make efforts (both in time and money) to co-operate in improving their property. Bulgarian rural areas are confronted with a large share of absentee-owners; owners who are not interested in the use of their land but only in its stable value. In addition, they are typically mistrusting toward any government interference in their property. So they do not co-operate in a project that costs money, has a risk of ending up in disputes and that has no apparent advantages at all.

These two complications yield a negative answer to the question whether Bulgaria needs land consolidation at all. In other Central European regions, like Southeast Poland, such serious obstructions to land consolidation are not present. And Bulgaria might outgrow these complications in the near future.

References

Benedek, J., 2000. Land reform in Romania after 1989: Towards market oriented agriculture? In: Tillack, P. and Schulze, E. (eds.) *Land Ownership, Land Markets and their Influence on the Efficiency of Agricultural Production in Central and Eastern Europe*, IAMO, Halle/Saale.

Land Fragmentation in Central Europe 47

Bisle, F., 1986. Teilnehmergemeinschaften. In: Magel, H. and Zehetmeier, A. (eds.), *100 Jahre Flurbereinigung in Bayern*, Bayerischen Staatsministerium für Ernährung, Landwirtschaft und Forsten, München.

Borek, T., 1993. Stand und Zukunft der polnischen Landwirtschaft. In: *Vermessung, Photogrammetrie*, Kulturtechnik 4/93.

Brooks, K.M., 1993, Property rights in land. In: Braverman, A., Brooks, K.M. and Csaki, C. (eds.) *The Agricultural Transition in Central and Eastern Europe and the Former USSR*, World Bank, Washington.

Creed, G.W., 1992. *Economic Development under Socialism: a Bulgarian Village on the Eve of Transition*, CUNY dissertation.

Davidova, S. and Buckwell, A., 2000. Transformation of Central and Eastern European agriculture and integration with the EU: progress and issues. In: Banse, M. and Tangermann, S. (eds.) *Central and Eastern European Agriculture in an Expanding European Union*, CABI Publishing, Wallingford.

Davidova, S., Buckwell, A. and Kopeva, D., 1997. Bulgaria: economics and politics of post-reform farm structures. In: Swinnen, J.F.M., *et al.* (eds.) *Agricultural Privatisation, Land Reform and Farm Restructuring in Central Europe*, Ashgate, Aldershot.

Dawson, A.H., 1984. *The Land Problem in the Developed Economy*, Croom Helm Ltd, Beckenham.

Dekker, H., 2001. *A New Property Regime in Kyrgystan: an Investigation into the Links between Land Reform, Food Security, and Economic Development*, University of Amsterdam.

Dingsdale, A., 1999. Redefining Eastern Europe: a new regional geography of post-socialist Europe? *Geography*, **3**, 204-221.

Harcsa, I. Kovách, I. and Szelényi, I., 1998. The price of privatisation. The post-communist transformational crisis of the Hungarian agrarian system. In: Szelényi, I. (ed.), *Privatising the Land. Rural Political Economy in Post-Communist Societies*, Routledge, London.

Kabat, L. and Hagedorn, K., 1997. Privatisation and decollectivisation policies and resulting structural changes of agriculture in Slovakia. In: Swinnen, J.F.M., *et al.* (eds.) *Agricultural Privatisation, Land Reform and Farm Restructuring in Central Europe*, Ashgate, Aldershot.

Lerman, Z., 2001. Agriculture in transition economies: from common heritage to divergence, *Agricultural Economics*, **26**, 95-114.

Mathijs, E. and Swinnen. J.F.M., 1996. *The Economics of Agricultural Decollectivisation in Central and Eastern Europe*, Policy Research Group, Working Paper No. 1, Leuven.

Meurs, M., 1999. *Many Shades of Red: State Policy and Collective Agriculture*, Rowman and Littlefield Inc., Maryland.

Pryor, F.L., 1992. *The Red and the Green: the Rise and Fall of Collectivised Agriculture in Marxist Regimes*, Princeton University Press, Princeton.

Schlögl, A., 1951. *Die Flurbereinigung in Bayern*, Bayerischer Landwirtschafts Verlag München.

Steuer, R., 1956. *Flurbereinigungsgesetz; Kommentar,* Beck, München.

Swinnen, J.F.M., 1996. *An Explanation of Land Reform Choices in Central and Eastern Europe*, Working Paper No. 5, Policy Research Group, Leuven.

Tillack, P. and Schulze, E. (eds.), 2000. *Land Ownership, Land Markets and their Influence on the Efficiency of Agricultural Production in Central and Eastern Europe*, Proceedings of the IAMO Seminar, Halle/Saale, Germany.

Van Dijk, T., 2002. Export of planning knowledge needs comparative analysis: the case of applying Western land consolidation knowledge in Central Europe, *European Planning Studies*, **7**, 913-924.

Van Lier, H., 2000. Van cultuurtechniek naar landgebruiksplanning en... terug: een slinger van Foucault? Valedictory address Wageningen University.

Voltr, V., 2000. EU accession and the land market in the Czech Republic. In: Tillack, P. and Schulze, E. (eds.), *Land Ownership, Land Markets and their Influence on the Efficiency of Agricultural Production in Central and Eastern Europe*, Proceedings of the IAMO Seminar, Halle/Saale, Germany.

Yin, R.K., 1994. *Case study research: design and methods*, Sage, London.

Zevenbergen, J.A., 2002. *Systems of Land Registration: Aspects and Effects*, Netherlands Geodetische Commissie, Delft.

Chapter 6

The Implementation Framework of Legal Systems

Ninel Jasmine Sadjadi

Introduction

A functioning land market is essential for the economic development of any country. In countries where private real property is permitted, the land market is an essential instrument, not only for the individual to gain a better living standard as he/she can sell/buy/mortgage his land, but also for the state as a whole. Land transactions not only bring direct income to the state, but also indirect income via a flourishing economy as many businesses depend on land (banking sector, property related professions, notaries, etc.).

Whereas in western countries the land market has developed by tradition, this tradition was interrupted in the CEE countries that followed the command economy. In these countries, no private real property existed (or hardly existed) and no transfer of such property meant a land market could not develop. There was no need for the development of provisions concerning, for example valuation, registration, and surveying of properties, mortgaging, etc. After the changes of 1990, these countries are now trying to establish a land market.[1] However, a functioning land market does not develop by its own, but gradually evolve over time. Therefore, the crucial question is what can be done to enhance the development of a functioning land market.[2]

The legal framework

When thinking of implementing new land systems like a new cadastre, new surveys, banks, etc., it is essential to realise that the quality and effectiveness of an emerging land market depends on the quality of the underlying legislation. The social life of humankind has been based on rules (of conduct) and on a legal order. Without any rules, society in general would not be where it stands. The quality of

---

[1] This includes Hungary, Poland, the Czech Republic, Slovenia, and the Slovak Republic, which have already developed considerable legislation on land law. Romania, Bulgaria, and the Russian Federation are in the process of doing so.
[2] See also the UN/ECE – Land Administration Guidelines (ECE/HBP/96).

50   *Methodologies, Models and Instruments*

the legislation ultimately influences the expected results; ineffective laws usually do not bring what they are expected to. There is no doubt that during the last thousands of years of human history, humankind has had sufficient time to develop many different legal systems, some of them more efficient than others.[3] Now we can look back at all these possibilities and try to best adapt them to our needs.

This is also true for the land market.[4] A functioning land market can only develop if the underlying legislation is well thought-out and specifically designed for the anticipated results. Therefore, the first important step for the implementation of new legislation is an analysis of the legal system employed by the respective country. Thus, deficiencies and backlogs of the current legislation can be defined and the country's needs be deduced thereof. Based on this, the aims to be achieved by the introduction of legislation can be identified. Special attention in this context should be made to the economic situation of a country, especially whether a country's economy is more agriculturally oriented or more industrially oriented, as this could be a special indicator for better understanding a country-specific land policy as well as for defining the actual needs of this country. To agriculturally oriented economies issues of enforcement of agriculture, livestock farming, crops, etc., are of different importance than to industrial economies, where focus is more on issues of development of new industrial, or service sectors. Of course, there will hardly be any purely agriculturally or purely industrially oriented countries, but most of them will follow a kind of mixed economy, as for example does Austria. It is also true that development goes towards industry gaining more and more importance, whilst agriculture is decreasing, although at the same time it has to be supported in order to secure the country's own agricultural production.[5]

As already mentioned, it is necessary to look at what kind of legislation already exists in the country and what is the country's legal tradition.[6] Here, however, not only the differences between Common Law and Civil Law countries need to be taken into account. We all know about the difficulties in implementation of for example Anglo-American instruments into traditionally Continental European influenced countries. What else needs to be realised is the fact that also

---

[3] See *Hudson/Levine*, Privatisation in the Ancient Near East and Classical Antiquity (1996); *Hudson/Levine*, Urbanization and Land Ownership in the Ancient Near East (1999).

[4] *Ibid.*

[5] Like many other countries also in Austria, agriculture needs to be supported by the state. It is further no secret that the European Union heavily subsidises European agriculture (Common Agricultural Policy - CAP). According to the OECD about 40% of the agricultural products are subsidised, see *Tangermann*, Mit einem Fuß auf dem Gaspedal, mit dem anderen auf der Bremse, Frankfurter Allgemeine Zeitung of February 26, 1999, page 11.

[6] See *David/Grasmann*, Einführung in die großen Privatrechtssysteme der Gegenwart (1998); *Merryman/Clark/Haley*, The Civil Law Tradition: Europe, Latin America and East Asia (1994), 213 ff; *Posch*, Grundzüge fremder Privatrechtssysteme (1995); *Zweigert/Kötz*, An Introduction to Comparative Law, 2nd ed (1987); *Zweigert/Kötz*, Einführung in die Rechtsvergleichung, 3. Aufl. (1996).

within Civil Law tradition we can look at various different sub-traditions, which have grown on different historical legal backgrounds. The Roman Law Tradition for example, comprising mainly France, Italy and Spain, but also Portugal, the Netherlands and parts of Latin America, is based on the French Civil Code, which is influenced by natural law.

The German legal tradition on the other hand is primarily based on the German Civil Code, which stands for a rather different approach to Civil law. Not only German speaking countries themselves, but also Greece, Turkey and Japan partly belong to the this German legal sub tradition, whilst Austria with its Civil Code of 1811 influenced by nature law stands in between the French and the German Civil Code. In addition, the Law of the Scandinavian countries has its own legal tradition and unrelated to either the German or the Anglo-American system.

Interestingly enough, the former Communist countries formed their own legal sub tradition, the so-called socialist legal tradition, which was naturally based on the ideas of Marx, Engels and Lenin. This sub tradition was interrupted after the changes of the revolutions and so far from a legal point of view, it is not yet clear how and in which direction these countries will develop.[7] They might become part of one of the existing legal traditions or they might form an own. In this context, of course European Law needs to be mentioned. Whether this legal tradition in the future will overlap with or override the existing legal traditions will be seen. From this we can see that it is important to take already existing legislation in a country as a given basis for future necessary changes.

In this context it might also be important to build up, if and where possible, on already developed legal instruments. Most of the countries have already developed definitions and principles, like definitions for property rights. So for example the principle of *superficies solo cedit* is not followed in many of the countries in transition, as for example Slovakia, Czech Republic, Russian Federation, and it has to be examined in each individual case whether its introduction would be useful or not. This shows that it is necessary sometimes to accept that due to the different legal tradition and due to different economic aims, definitions, and principles might vary from one country to the other.

This leads to another aspect, namely the acceptance of legal instruments by the population, which is tightly bound to the legal tradition just mentioned, as the implementation of systems that are not in line with traditionally grown principles is often very difficult if it happens without the acceptance of the concerned people. This usually leads to non-compliance with laws and ultimately to their total ineffectiveness together with the development of new 'undercover' systems that have no legal justification, but function due to social acceptance. One reason for this might also be the factual costs of transactions of real property. If they are too high, people will find ways to circumvent the legal provisions.

A further issue, quite related to the acceptance by the population, of course is legal safety. People must trust in the system, this is only possible if the system

---

[7] For example, there is no notion on the socialist or former socialist legal tradition in the third edition of *Zweigert/Kötz,* Einführung in die Rechtsvergleichung, 3. Aufl. (1996), whereas it used to be explained in the two previous editions of 1969 and 1984.

52   *Methodologies, Models and Instruments*

can keep its guarantees. This for example refers to the factual existence of real property titles, as well as to the security for mortgage lenders (banks) to get back their investments in case the mortgagee goes bankrupt.

Another fact to be kept in mind is transparency of the system. The whole land law system can only function properly if people have sufficient access to information, i.e., if they can see the registers and inform themselves about the legal status of the real property in question.

But where now to begin when trying to establish new land legislation in a country? A country's legal order usually follows a hierarchical structure, with the constitution as the highest and most important law to be followed.[8] The constitution not only contains the aims and ideas a country stands for, but also outlines the general structures of a state system. Thus, for example in the constitution we find the fundamental rights a country is willing to protect. Whether private real property is permitted for the individual, whether the right to be heard is accepted in judicial procedure, whether separation of powers is a principle accepted by the state, whether restitution is an aim and whether this should happen with or without compensation, all this can be taken from the constitution. The constitution is the highest law of every state and any changes of the legal order have to comply with the principles set out in the constitution.

In this context, the international treaties ratified by the respective country have to be taken into consideration. The provisions that are in force and their relation to the constitution have to be defined. Usually within the hierarchical structure of the legal system, international treaties are considered to have the same level than the constitution has. Some of them even become a part of the constitution, as for example, the Human Rights Convention (HRC)[9] sometimes does, which for property rights is of special interest as it contains the definition of property rights and their guarantee by state. Especially in regard of CEE countries the status of negotiations with the European Union are of importance. How far have negotiations proceeded so far?[10] Is there already any sort of EC-legislation

---

[8] This is also true for Scandinavian law (see *Ring/Olsen-Ring*, Einführung in das skandinavische Recht [1999], 32 ff) and for Spanish law, where the constitution of 1978 was first changed in the course of the EU-Maastricht treaty (see *Adomeit/Frühbeck*, Einführung in das spanische Recht [1993], 44; for the hierarchical structure in Austria see *Walter/Mayer*, Grundriß des österreichischen Bundesverfassungsrechts (1996), 62ff and *Öhlinger*, Verfassungsrecht, 4th ed (1999)25 ff. Whereas in Austria constitutional provisions can be changed by other constitutional provisions with a two-third majority, in Germany a change of certain provisions of the so-called Grundgesetz is not possible (so-called 'Ewigkeitsklausel'; see *Öhlinger*, Vergleichendes Verfassungsrecht [1991] 53ff); England has no written constitution. The laws that comprise the usual content of a constitution are not binding there for the Parliament, therefore it can be held that no typical hierarchical structure of the legislation can be found in the UK (see *Blumenwitz*, Einführung in das anglo-amerikanische Recht [1998] 18.

[9] See: http://www.dhdirhr.coe.fr/intro/eng/GENERAL/ECHR.HTM.

[10] This is especially important for the countries of the first Accession Round: Poland, Hungary, the Czech Republic, and Slovenia.

The Implementation Framework of Legal Systems   53

that has to be taken into account when drafting new legislation? What about the pre-accession treaties?

Below the level of the constitution, we find federal laws and regulations that apply to the country as a whole. These laws and regulations can be substantive ones governing special topics, but they can also be adjective ones containing provisions relating to the distribution of competencies and responsibilities among the various institutions existing in the country[11] as well as to procedural aspects. Below this level, there can be several more levels of regional and communal legislation, each of which depends on all the upper levels' legislation.

Adjective aspects - institutions

The implementation of land related laws usually lies with state institutions - as opposed to private institutions. Therefore, an analysis must take place about which institutions are entrusted with the implementation and whether - especially with regard to institutional conflicts, which are commonly found in countries in transition - such conflicts are to be feared. As land is a so-called cross-sectoral issue[12] this examination, as will be shown below, has to be carried out on a horizontal level as well as on a vertical level.

Land related laws usually involve various different authorities at different levels. At the ministry level, usually the Ministry of Agriculture is involved as well as the Ministry of Justice and the Ministry of Finance. In Romania, for example, the Ministry of Public Works has additional competencies and in the Russian Federation it is the Ministry of Industry, Science and Technology. Cadastre issues are often, as in Austria, dealt with under the jurisdiction of the Ministry of Economics and Labour. Under the jurisdiction of each Ministry, it might be possible to establish several different kinds of authorities and institutions, all dealing solely or partly also with land issues. In Romania, again we find 42 District Rural Cadastre Offices, which are under the competence of the Ministry of Agriculture, so called Cadastre Offices for agricultural Land Organisation (OCAOTA), which are in charge of issuing property titles. On the other hand there is the National Office of Cadastre, Geodesy and Cartography (National Cadastre Office - NCO)[13] created under the jurisdiction of the Prime Minister's office that has 42 Local General Cadastral Offices (LGCO).

---

[11] See the national Laws on the Establishment and Powers of Ministries (in Austria for example: Bundesministeriengesetz 1986).

[12] For cross-sectoral issues in Austria see *Walter/Mayer*, Grundriß des österreichischen Bundesverfassungsrechts (1996), marginal number 301, 853, and 1090 and *Öhlinger*, Verfassungsrecht, 4th ed (1999), 129.

[13] The *NCO* is an independent agency, which was created in November 1996. It is financed partly through the national budget and partly through fees that are charged for services. At the current time, there is no electronic data interchange between the regional offices and the head office although this is planned for the future.

An example for conflicts on the vertical line are those between legislators of different levels in federally organised countries, i.e., conflicts between the federal, the state or the regional legislators over their competencies. A very famous example for this is Italy.[14]

There might also be commonly (i.e. under the jurisdiction of two or more ministries) established institutions or institutions having a special mandate for specific issues. All these structures need to be identified before starting to develop new legislation. Therefore, it is of utmost importance not only to look at the horizontal distribution of powers, but also pay attention to the relevant vertical aspects of distribution of powers. Which powers do laws give to which authorities of which level? How does the co-ordination and co-operation of these authorities work? Are there any provisions for this? Is there any potential of conflicts in the interplay between federal, regional, communal and possibly further state levels? Another factor of course is bureaucracy within the authorities. Procedures usually and especially in land related issues take very long. An important and delicate issue in this context is the probability of corruption within the authorities.[15]

In case new national authorities are to be established the usefulness and effectiveness, in regards to the hazard potential of institutional conflicts, of this step, must be carefully analysed. What especially needs to be identified is whether the creation of new authorities could be substituted by (cost saving) restructuring measures among already existing institutions, or even by creation of just additional responsibilities within existing structures. Part of the examination also has to be the estimation and assessment of the expected implementation costs of the draft law (creation of additional authorities, and jobs, etc.).

The legislation and execution of land law due to its cross sectional character has as its consequence not only the involvement of various institutions, but should also be understood as a complex collection of numerous interconnected qualities differing in accordance with the respective national structures. Therefore, an analysis of the legal fields related or directly connected with the law that is to be implemented and the degree of changes necessary within these provisions (and if so, in which relation) will have to be made. In this connection, it also needs to be analysed whether the changes are complete and coherent.

The role of legal professions must also be considered. For example, to what extent officials within the state authorities should be independent and/or irremovable in order to be able to better process applications? In Austria, for example, much importance is attached to the fact that all issues related to the registration of titles are dealt with by the courts, whilst in many other countries (especially the Slovak and Czech Republics) following the unified cadastre these functions are carried out by civil servants within the administrative bodies.

Private legal professions should not be neglected: notaries for example are usually in charge of all transaction issues as therefore a notarial deed is necessary.

---

[14] For a recent contribution to the Italian case see 'Italiens endlose Föderalismus-Debatte' in Neue Züricher Zeitung of November 18./19., 2000.

[15] For institutional problems, also see *Palmer*, Making Land Registration More Effective (http://www.fao.org/DOCREP/X3720t/x3720t04.htm).

The Implementation Framework of Legal Systems 55

In addition, they are usually responsible for handling registration issues. Lawyers of course play an important role as the individual usually lacks legal information, which he tries to overcome by consultation with a lawyer.

Here, also, the training needs for such professionals need to be identified in order to develop an appropriate educational programme. Other important private professions, in the context of land issues, are for example private licensed surveyors (as individual landowners who want to sell their property usually have to have it surveyed) as well as real property agents, valuation experts and banking professions.

Substantive aspects - environment

Just as institutional aspects generally form a certain background to the implementation of any new legal systems and laws, some substantive aspects such as environmental issues also have the same effect. Problems of waste management, air pollution, preservation of nature and the like will be of growing importance in the future. Legal systems when being implemented will in future have to take into consideration a country's underlying policies and decisions concerning the environment as well as international treaties on environmental topics. The United Nations has already tried to increase awareness of this topic on several conferences.[16] The European Union has issued several Directives and Resolutions on environment.[17] Furthermore, those projects proposed for funding by the World Bank also requires environmental assessment by potential borrowers.[18] In 1989, the Bank established a specific policy and procedures for environmental assessment

---

[16] World Climate Conferences in Geneva in 1979 and 1990; Toronto Conference on the Changing Atmosphere in 1988 calling for a 20% reduction of global CO_2 emissions by 2005; Conference of the Parties of the UN-Framework Convention on Climate Change (FCCC) in Berlin (1995) and Kyoto (1997); UN Conference on Environment and Development in Rio de Janeiro (1992) reaffirming the declaration made at the UN Conference on the Human Environment in Stockholm (1972) (Rio-Declaration); Principle 4 of the Rio-Declaration holds: 'In order to achieve sustainable development, environmental protection shall constitute an integral part of the development process and cannot be considered in isolation from it'.

[17] See for example Council Resolution of 3 March 1975 on energy and the environment, *OJ C 168 25.07.1975 p.2;* Council Directive 85/337/EEC of 27 June 1985 on the assessment of the effects of certain public and private projects on the environment, *OJ L 175 05.07.1985 p.40;* Council Directive 75/442/EEC of 15 July 1975 on waste, *OJ L 194 25.07.1975 p.39;* Council Resolution of 7 May 1990 on waste policy, *OJ C 122 18.05.1990 p.2;* Council Resolution of 15 December 1998 on a forestry strategy for the European Union, *OJ C 056 26.02.1999 p.1*; Special Report No 3/98 concerning the implementation by the Commission of EU policy and action as regards water pollution accompanied by the replies of the Commission (Pursuant to the second indent of paragraph 4 of Article 188c of the EC-Treaty), *OJ C 191 18.06.1998, p.2; for further information see http://europa.eu.int/eur-lex/en/lif/reg/en_register_151010.html.*

[18] See the World Bank Monthly Operational Summary (MOS).

56 *Methodologies, Models and Instruments*

and related environmental analyses of IBRD and IDA lending operations.[19] In 1991, the Bank revised its policies and procedures so that projects are now assigned to categories based upon the nature, magnitude, and sensitivity of environmental issues. Awareness of the importance of this factor has definitely grown already, but is this sufficient? Does the legislator take it into account when making a new law and does the addressee of the respective law adhere to it?

Substantive aspects - land legislation

As far as the substantive aspects of land legislation are concerned, it is essential to define the outcomes of such action.[20] The land market means the interaction of an uncountable number of different fields. Only if there are legal provisions for all of them can they interact properly and allow a fully functioning land market to evolve. It is, therefore, necessary to look at all aspects of the relevant legislation involved since land markets and land law involve a much broader spectrum of fields. Concepts for single land-related reforms such as, housing provisions, bankruptcy and mortgage laws, land lease provisions, or property tax laws, etc., cannot be seen as isolated issues but, from a legal point of view, have to be viewed as part of the whole framework on land (related) issues. They need to be developed within a broader framework that also addresses problems of inheritance law, off-land job opportunities for farmers, urban planning, village renovation, and the whole urban and rural development, as well as being in accordance with the country's core provisions on land registration, cadastre, land consolidation, valuation, and other land related legislation.

In addition, other factors to be taken into consideration include:

- how could land be best surveyed in order to get the best results at minimum costs?
- how should a cadastre be designed?
- how can plots be rightly valued?
- should titles be provided to land owners?
- should registration work?
- the mortgaging system;
- the fees involved with transactions;
- what should be the state income? and
- how should dispute adjudication be regulated?

---

[19] Under this environmental assessment process, the type, timing, and main issues of environmental analysis to be performed by the borrower are to be confirmed at the time that a given lending operation is initiated into the World Bank's prospective lending program and thereafter reported and updated on a quarterly basis in the MOS.

[20] General on Land Legislation in Austria see *Walter/Mayer,* Grundriß des besonderen Verwaltungsrecht (1987), 224ff; *Raschauer,* Allgemeines Verwaltungsrecht (1998) marginal numbers 294, 305, and 432.

In relation to CEE countries, provisions of restitution[21] and privatisation are of special importance, as they present the legal precondition for any following land legislation. This is also true for issues of state owned land and expropriation issues as well as sufficient measures to keep land fragmentation at a tolerable level.

New land related provisions must, therefore, only be implemented with regard to all the related provisions in order to prevent inconsistencies in legislation. Special attention must also be paid to transitory provisions, as they often serve as a breeding-ground for institutional conflicts.

When implementing new systems it is, therefore, of outmost importance to take care that these new systems are consistent within themselves. Different legal instruments are usually characterised by different legal principles that adhere to them. So for example a title registration system is usually characterised by a constitutive registration i.e., the property right only comes into existence with the very registration. This is not so with the deeds registration system, where the contractual agreement is the important factor.[22]

In this context of course, the issue of duties and fees is an overall important one. On the one hand, taxes on real property and fees in connection with transactions constitute a part of the state income. On the other hand, if duties and fees are too high landowners might be deprived of any incentive to act according to legal provisions. Therefore, in Romania for example there used to be no income tax on property transactions, which will change with effect from January 1, 2001. Transactions and other legally important actions might then happen out of the sphere of the law making authorities. If this proves to be unacceptable by the majority of the population, the newly introduced systems will be ineffective. The described picture shows, that the main problems in the implementation of new laws and systems i.e., the institutional problems, as well as the general policy considerations, will remain the same even if the actual topic to be regulated changes. Therefore, the solution of these problems will be the same independent of the substantive content of the new legislation. The essence of all this is that the various laws, those that are already in place and those going to be implemented, need to be substantively coherent and have to interlock with each other.

Substantive aspects - water and forest related legislation

What has been said in the context of land related legislation is applicable to nearly any sort of legislation to be implemented. An issue for example of rising interest in the near future will be water. Here as well, different interests of different authorities

---

[21] For expropriation and restitution in East Germany see *Redeker*, Zehn Jahre Wiedervereinigung – Bewältigung eigentums- und vermögensrechtlicher Fragen, NJW 2000, Heft 41. For the situation on property rights in Hungary and Croatia see *Borić*, Eigentum und Privatisierung in Kroatien und Ungarn (1996), 27 ff.

[22] For a classification of registration systems see *Palmer*, Making Land Registration More Effective (http://www.fao.org/DOCREP/X3720t/x3720t04.htm); in detail see *Gravells*, Land law, 2nd ed (1999), 105ff.

will have to be co-ordinated. Furthermore, as with land related provisions, many different aspects of substantive law are interwoven here, too. Problems of shrinking water resources on the one hand, pollution of rivers, lakes, and the sea or contamination of ground water, are just a few aspects. The same is true for forestry or protection of nature.

Conclusion

The described picture shows how difficult the introduction of an entire legal framework for a specific substantive legal field can be. However, the task can become easier through the use of a common database, to which the responsible authorities have specifically tailored access, i.e. a real property database might be used for title registration as well as for cadastre information or tax information. Each authority will then have access to the information, and only to the information, it needs in order to deal with the respective case. Such databases would not only help to save costs, but would also serve for more transparency in the system, for less failures by the authorities due to wrong information and thus to acceleration of procedures and eventually, if the a state so decides, one stop shopping for the customer.

More important however is the fact that such complex and interconnected legislation cannot be implemented in a country in one single step, but has to split into several 'legislative packages', which according to the respective country's needs, in a step-by-step development, introduces the relevant legislation. This again might be easier if pilot areas were defined where the said legislation can be implemented first and where, within a certain time, experiences can be collected that might be helpful when implementing the legislation in the whole country.

Chapter 7

Mediation in Land Consolidation and in Boundary Disputes

Jørn Rognes and Per Kåre Sky

Introduction

Mediation, in general, is gaining popularity as a dispute resolution technique (Kressel and Pruitt, 1989), and there is increasing interest to its application in planning and land use disputes (Rubino and Jacobs, 1990). Mediation, it is argued, can be efficient (Wall and Rude, 1991) and can produce high quality settlements (Galanter, 1985). There is, however, limited knowledge concerning the practice of mediation in land use disputes and in land consolidation, when mediation should be used, the results achieved, and how mediation activities are carried out.

The land consolidation court in Norway is a particularly useful setting for studying mediation with regard to land issues. Land consolidation is organised within the judicial system. The jurisdiction of the courts includes both land consolidation planning and the solving of boundary disputes. Any disputes concerning boundaries, rights of ownership, rights of users, or other matters, is decided by the judgment of the land consolidation court if it is necessary for the purpose of land consolidation.

This chapter, based on the hypothesis that mediation plays a dominant role in judges' activities during the average court session, is organised in three stages. Firstly, a short overview of the functions of the land consolidation courts in Norway is given. Secondly, the relevant theory on mediation is discussed, and thirdly, a study investigated by the authors is presented and the results are documented. Finally, the implications of findings for the mediation of land consolidation and boundary disputes are discussed.

Land consolidation in Norway

In Norway, land consolidation is a permanent public institution, entirely within the framework of the judicial system. Norway is the only European country that has organised its land consolidation process completely within the framework of its judicial system. In each particular case, the land consolidation court is composed of one land consolidation judge acting as a president, and two duly appointed lay judges.

The decisions are reached by a vote among the judges present. To practice as a land consolidation judge, one must have a Masters degree from the Agricultural University of Norway. Normally the degree will study a number of relevant subjects, including surveying, mapping, cadastre, law, and land consolidation.

Land consolidation is normally carried out for all the holdings in a specific, geographically limited - but defined - area. The size and scope of land consolidation varies from minor adjustments of boundaries between two holdings, to complete rearrangement of hundreds of holdings, with planning and investments in new infrastructure. At a fundamental level, the land consolidation process is intended to restructure outdated or unsatisfactory ownership patterns. Any landed property that is considered difficult to utilise efficiently under existing circumstances may be subjected to land consolidation under the terms of the Land Consolidation Act. The same applies when circumstances become unfavourable as a result of building, improvement, maintenance, and the operation of public roads, including the closing down of private railways (Land Consolidation Act, § 1, hereinafter referred to by section number).

It is necessary to provide in some detail the specific subject matter of what land consolidation in Norway may comprise (§ 2), since the questionnaire that formed the basis of this study was drawn directly from different articles in this section. Land consolidation may comprise:

§ 2a) dissolving a system of joint ownership under which land or rights are jointly owned by estates;

§ 2b) reallocating landed property through the exchange of land;

§ 2c) prescribing rules relating to the use of any area that is subject to joint use by estates, or prescribing rules relating to the use of any area that is not subject to joint use by estates when the land consolidation court finds that the attendant circumstances make such use particularly difficult;

§ 2d) eliminating outdated rights of use, and assigning compensation;

§ 2e) organizing such joint measures as mentioned in the Land Act (measuring for agricultural purposes), and in the Act relating to water resources (measuring for draining);

§ 2f) reallocating landed properties when land and rights are to be disposed of in accordance with the purpose of Land Act;

§ 2g) dividing a landed property with the rights pertaining to it in accordance with a specific scale of values;

§ 2h) clarifying and determining conditions relating to property and rights of use under joint ownership and in other areas that are subject to joint use by estates when this is necessary with a view to a rational use of the area.

Another type of case that can be handled in the land consolidation court covers the delimitation of boundaries (§ 88). An owner may request the land consolidation court in a specific case to clarify, mark, and describe the boundaries of his property and the boundaries for perpetual rights of use. This type of case represents between 40% and 50% of all cases handled in the court each year. The owner has the right to choose to bring these types of cases to the ordinary courts, or to the land consolidation court. Mostly, these cases are brought to the latter for the following reasons:

- the case has not developed into a real dispute in the legal sense, such that it should be brought to the ordinary court;
- the legal situation regarding the land is obscure, and one of the owners wants an independent institution to investigate the matter;
- the land consolidation court procedure has the benefit that parties need not be represented by a lawyer;
- the land consolidation court has the technical equipment and competence that is needed for all the cadastral work that typically follows upon a verdict of the court.

This is not true of the ordinary courts. After a verdict in a boundary dispute in the ordinary courts the parties have to request a survey from the surveying department in the municipality (Sevatdal, 1986).

The land consolidation courts follow normal court procedure for all kinds of decisions, even in matters such as valuation and physical planning. This procedure is well known and generally accepted. The land consolidation process can be outlined in the following main stages:

- applying for land consolidation;
- decision whether the case shall proceed;
- clarifying the boundaries and mapping of the consolidation area;
- valuation of anything that is subject to the exchange;
- preparation of a draft consolidation plan;
- presentation of the plan to the parties for discussion;
- comments from the parties;
- alteration on the basis of comments on the plan that the court deems right and proper;
- formal adoption of the plan; marking out of all new boundaries in the fields; and the
- formal conclusion of the land consolidation proceeding in court.

Land consolidation cannot be effective if the costs and disadvantages involved exceed the benefits accruing to each individual property (§ 3a).

The overall aim for land consolidation, if boundary disputes or land disputes (§ 88 and § 2h) are omitted, is to increase the net income from the holding. This might be obtained either through increasing the volume of production or by lowering the cost of production. Mediation is a very important activity during the phase in the process, in which the land consolidation court draws up the draft

62 *Methodologies, Models and Instruments*

consolidation plan for presentation to, and discussion with, the parties. This is also emphasised in the Land Consolidation Act (§ 20) whereby the court shall draw up a draft consolidation plan, which shall be presented for the parties for discussion. The land consolidation court shall also consult with the public authorities if the consolidation plan is likely to affect matters within their jurisdiction. The main emphasis of the Land Consolidation Act is that the court should first utilise mediation in the case of boundary disputes before a prospective trail.

Mediation

In contrast to most judges, the land consolidation judge is an expert on the substantive issues of the disputes and, in contrast to most mediators, the land consolidation judge can adjudicate decisions if needed. Therefore, based on his knowledge and experience the judge must decide when and how intensively to mediate the case, and how to behave as a mediator. Theory related to each of these roles in turn will be discussed.

When to mediate

To understand mediation in land consolidation proceedings, the study of judicial decision-making processes, particularly those that investigate the judge's role as a mediator in court, is a good starting point. The literature on judicial mediation (see generally Galanter, *op cit.*; Schiller and Wall, 1981; Wall and Rude, 1989; and Wall, Rude and Schiller, 1984) is generally enthusiastic for it to be applied by the courts because it reduces backlog, whilst the mediated decisions are often perceived as more satisfying than a judicial decree. Mediated settlement yield many benefits for the disputing parties, including reduced costs compared to a full trial, the potential for better relationships between the parties in the future, and the fact that the parties have greater control over the course of the case. However, Tomasic (1980) makes a critical comparison of mediation and court processing. He uses the findings of the Vera Institute in Brooklyn, that the difference in 'experienced fairness' between a mediation and trial was smaller than might have been expected. Furthermore, the disputing parties occasionally want an outside agency to make a decision for them. A critical issue for land consolidation judges is, therefore, when to apply mediation and when to serve primarily in an adjudicative capacity.

In choosing a decision-making procedure, the judge can mediate, adjudicate, or combine the two procedures. Combination of the two procedures can either be in a mediation-adjudication process, where the judge first mediates and, if mediation is unsuccessful, then adjudicates. Alternatively, the judge can mediate some issues and adjudicate others, which is probably the most likely solution in complex land-use planning cases.

All participants in the mediation process are influenced by awareness that the court has the power to make the final decision (Pruitt and Kressel, 1985). Unlike most third parties, judges who mediate are more powerful than either of the two disputants; for this reason they are free to employ as many techniques and be as assertive as they wish (Wall and Rude, *op cit.*).

The power and the freedom in the choice of decision-making process make the judge a very active and creative mediator. However, the focus on neutrality, the participant's rights to have a third party decision, together with the challenges associated with the same person both mediating and judging may hinder willingness to mediate. How the mediator balances these opposing forces should be reflected in behavioural variations across different type of cases.

Wall *et al.* (1984) analysed the attempts of judges to settle simple and complex cases. They matched case size with case complexity to form four, 2-variable pairings: *small and simple, small and complex,* large and simple, *large and complex.* In three of the four of these pairings (in italics), the judge actively facilitated settlement.

Mediation behaviour

Mediation is a generic term covering a wide range of behavioural styles and techniques (Kressel and Pruitt, *op cit.*). In general mediation facilitated negotiation (Kovach, 1994), in those cases in which the mediator assisted the disputing parties in trying to voluntarily reach a settlement (Moore, 1996). It is a highly adaptive and responsive process (Kolb, 1997) where the mediators vary their tactics and techniques with the nature of the conflict (Shapiro *et al.,*1985). Schiller and Wall (1981) identified 71 different techniques used by state judges and federal trial judges. Wall and Rude (1989) divide the mediation techniques into four strategic styles: logical strategies; aggressive strategies; paternalistic strategies, and client-oriented strategies. A logical strategy may involve analysing the case to develop and present alternative proposals. An aggressive strategy involves pressuring the parties, talking to them separately and downgrading the merits of the strongest case. A paternalistic strategy may involve recommending compromises, informing about risks going to a trial and channelling discussion towards manageable issues. Finally, a client-oriented strategy involves educating the parties and speaking personally to them. As judges in land consolidation courts are highly skilled experts on the conflictive issues, it is expected that they use general, logical strategies. There are differences of opinions as to whether the judge should actively promote settlements, and within the study it was expected to find differences in behaviour across judges in the Norwegian context. Finally, given that there are a variety of available techniques for mediation, and that the land consolidation judges have no formal training in mediation it was expected to find a considerable amount of variations both in preferences for mediation and in behavioural strategies.

The study

The empirical study had two major parts: a survey of cases handled in the court in 1996 and in depth interviews with judges regarding mediation behaviour.

The survey

An important part of research material is comprised of responses from judges in the land consolidation courts to a questionnaire related to mediation activity in all cases closed in 1996. Answers were received for 727 cases out of 992 possible (73%) from 91 judges in the land consolidation courts. The questionnaire contained eight questions for each case, and had to be returned together with official statistics for each case. The Land Consolidation Services collect and store data for each of the cases handled by the courts. They collect data, for example, on the type of case, information about the judge, the number of parties, area covered, length of the boundaries, etc. In this chapter six out of eight questions are discussed:

- *Question No. 1* investigates the intensity of the controversy between the parties in the case. The question had to be answered by checking one of five possibilities on a scale ranging from 'not to a very large degree' to 'very large degree'. The other possibilities were 'not to a large degree', 'to some degree', and 'to a large degree'. In the statistical analysis the answers are transformed into a five-point bipolar scale, where 'not to a very large degree' = 1 and 'to a very large degree' = 5;
- *Question No. 2* had four sub questions related to how decisions were reached. It was asked (a) how many verdicts were given in the case, (b) how many mediated settlements were reached, (c) how many agreements reached outside the court and (d) whether there was 'formless agreement' in the court. A 'formless agreement' means that the parties agreed on the issues in the case and the judge, therefore, writes in the court protocol that the parties have agreed in this way;
- *Question No. 3* should give information how many times the land consolidation plan was presented to the parties;
- *Questions No. 4 and No. 5* asked to what degree the parties had objected to the plan the first and the last time, respectively, it was presented. The scale used for this question was the same as for question 1; and, finally in
- *Question No. 6* the judge should estimate how much time was spent on mediation in the case. The possible answers were 'no mediation', 'less than two hours', 'two-five hours', 'five-eight hours' and 'more than eight hours'.

Mediation in Land Consolidation and in Boundary Disputes 65

In the statistical analysis we transformed the answers into a five-point bipolar scale, where 'no mediation or negotiation' = 1 and 'more than eight hours' = 5. The data are analysed simply by comparing means, and by using t-tests and correlations as statistical tests for differences and relationships. Firstly, differences between types of cases, and then investigated variations in mediation activities were examined. Finally, cases that are resolved through a trial were compared with those cases settled through mediation.

Differences between types of cases

Every land consolidation case has one *main means or type of dispute*, after one of the sections described earlier (§2a to §2h, or §88). In Table 7.1 the judges' answers were classified according to the main means.

It should be mentioned that a case might include several means to resolve the dispute. For example, in cases where the plots of the farms are fragmented the judges often use § 2b for the consolidation of the plots, and § 88 if there are any disputes about the boundaries of the plots that are to be consolidated. There are also considerable differences in the amount of controversy encountered across case types.

Table 7.1 Type of case in the land consolidation court, number of cases, mean controversy between the parties and standard deviations

Type of case	Number of cases[1]	Mean	(st.d)
§ 2 a	36	3.00	(1.15)
§ 2 b	76	2.12	(1.35)
§ 2 c	43	3.88	(1.07)
§ 2 d	20	3.30	(1.34)
§ 2 e	66	3.80	(1.04)
§ 2 f	53	1.75	(1.02)
§ 2 g	75	1.96	(1.19)
§ 2 h	46	4.04	(0.87)
§ 88	277	3.36	(1.28)

[1] *The number of cases varies a little among the different questions because of missing values in the questionnaire.*

Most controversies were found in cases dealing with clarifying and determining the conditions relating to property and the rights of the use under joint ownership, and in other areas that are subject to joint use by estates (§ 2h). Cases that prescribe rules relating to the use of any areas subject to joint use by estates, or prescribe rules to the use of any area that is not subject to joint use by estates when the court finds that the attendant circumstances make such use particularly difficult (§ 2c). Furthermore, joint measures (§ 2e) also have a high mean of controversy

66 *Methodologies, Models and Instruments*

between the parties. All of these types of cases comprise activities of joint use, measure, or ownership. Cases with individual property ownership are less controversial.

Throughout a land consolidation case, drafts of the plan are presented for the consideration of those involved. *Number of presentations* was used as a study variable. Presenting and redrafting plans are important mediation activities, and indicate an interactive process between mediator (judge) and the parties. The frequency of these presentations across cases was measured. It was found that in those cases of organising joint measures (§ 2e) the frequency of presentations was highest, with an average of 1.58 presentations per case. The second highest were cases of dissolving joint ownership (§ 2a), with an average of 1.39 presentations per case. Third and fourth highest were cases with eliminating outdated rights of use, and assigning compensation (§ 2d), and reallocating landed property through the exchange of land (§ 2b) with respectively 1.4 and 1.1 presentations per case on average. Cases organising joint measures are often cases involving financial investments. In considering whether the investments shall be made, the land consolidation court attaches importance to the future utilisation of the properties. That could be one of the reasons for the high frequency of presentations.

The judges were asked to estimate the amount of time used on mediation in different type of cases. Table 7.2 illustrates three types of case that have more mediation activity than others: dissolving joint ownership (§ 2a); prescription of rules relating to joint use of an area, or if the use of any area is particularly difficult (§ 2c); and the organisation of joint measures (§ 2e). All of these types of cases often have many parties, together with a comprehensive and complicated valuation process. On average, § 2a cases have 10.5 parties, § 2c cases have 19.5 parties, and § 2e cases have 14.4 parties. Each instance is greater than the average case, which was calculated to feature 8.3 parties. Joint measure-cases are often cases involving investments, such as the construction of roads).

Table 7.2   The extent of mediation and standard deviation sorted by type of case

Type of case	Number of cases	Mean	(st.d)
§ 2 a	37	3.22	(1.32)
§ 2 b	74	2.62	(1.44)
§ 2 c	40	3.48	(1.22)
§ 2 d	21	2.95	(1.32)
§ 2 e	67	3.52	(1.21)
§ 2 f	53	2.30	(1.44)
§ 2 g	75	2.05	(1.14)
§ 2 h	46	3.02	(1.32)
§ 88	277	2.70	(1.09)

In summary, the analyses related to case types revealed the following pattern. Most controversies were found in those cases comprising activities of joint use or joint measures. The frequency of presentations of plans was highest in cases with joint measures. Three types of cases had more mediation activity; dissolving joint ownership, prescription of rules relating to joint use of an area, or an area of particularly difficult use, and cases organising joint measures.

Other causes of mediation activity

It was shown that mediation activity varies with case type. In addition, correlation analysis showed that when there was high amount of controversy, the parties had many objections to the first plan presented by the judge ($r = 0.80$; $p<0.0001$). Consequently, it led to the judge developing several new drafts of the consolidation plan for presentation to the parties ($r = 0.44$; $p<0.0001$). Thus, comments and controversy generate high mediation activity in land planning disputes. The judge had some success in mediation because the parties had considerably fewer objections to the final plan presented than to the initial plan (means are 2.02 and 2.49, respectively, $t = 4.21$; $p<0.001$). In cases with high degrees of controversy, the parties often had objections to the final plan ($r = 0.50$; $p<0.0001$), even if those objections were fewer than for the first plan. The results also show that lawyers more often represented the parties in high controversy cases (mean = 4.12) than in low controversy cases (mean = 2.71). The difference is significant ($t = 15.50$, df = 690, $p<0.001$).

The trend in the data is that the time used on mediation and negotiation increases with the number of parties in the case. The correlation analysis also shows a positive relationship between the number of parties and the extent of mediation ($r = 0.26$; $p<0.0001$). The reason for the increase in mediation activity may be the complexity that multiparty cases represent.

How does the size of the consolidated area affect mediation? The correlation analysis showed that there was a positive relation ($r = 0.22$; $p<0.0001$) between the size of the consolidated area and the controversy. There was also a positive correlation ($r = 0.18$; $p<0.0009$) between the size of the area and the time spent on mediation.

In summary, the results show that mediation activities increase with the degree of controversy in the case, with the size of land under consideration, and with the number of parties involved.

Mediated settlements versus verdicts

Out of 786 decisions in the court, 42% involved verdicts and 58% were mediated settlements or agreements reached outside the court (in both land consolidation cases and boundary disputes). Almost half of the verdicts were in cases where the main means or type of disputes were boundary disputes.

68   *Methodologies, Models and Instruments*

In order to examine relationships between decision type (verdicts versus mediated settlement) and case characteristics, those cases under section § 2h and § 88 were investigated in more detail: 58 cases were settled through mediation and 110 cases with a trial and verdict. The mean level of controversy was significantly lower in cases with mediated outcome than in those with verdicts (mean level of controversy 3.66 and 4.25, respectively; t = 2.04 (df = 164), p<0.05). In cases settled through mediation the judge used marginally more time on mediation activities than on cases that ended with a verdict (means are 3.02 and 2.73 respectively; t = 1.76 (df = 165), p<0.10). Furthermore cases settled through mediation had fewer parties (on average 4.3 versus 7.8) and were smaller (in terms of length of boundary) then those that ended with verdicts. Finally, the parties were less frequently represented by lawyers (13.7% versus 22.3%).

Thus, the results show that mediated results are most often achieved in cases with limited amounts of controversy, low complexity (in terms of parties) and low significance (size of area and length of boundary). The judges spent only marginally more time on mediation in those cases ending with a mediated settlement than those ending with a verdict.

Interviews about mediation behaviour

The second part of the study involved in-depth interviews with 23 land consolidation judges concerning their experiences in mediation in the courts. The aim of the study was to establish the mediation strategies employed by the judges and evaluate how active they could be as mediators without threatening their role as judge in the case. Mediation behaviour was examined separately for both boundary disputes and land consolidation planning cases.

A general finding was the considerable difference in mediation activity between judges. This is surprising given that the Act recommends mediation in boundary disputes and requires it in planning issues, but does not specify mediation techniques. There is no formal training in mediation for judges. Their choice of behaviour is therefore up to their own discretion within the general boundaries of the judicial system. Some judges act intensively as deal-makers in the court using an extensive range of tactics, whilst varying their techniques across cases. Other judges were more careful, taking on a passive mediation role and only proposing mediated settlement when the stakes were low. The passive mediators argued that it was inappropriate to mediate extensively, given their role as judge, if mediated settlement was not reached.

Judicial pressure, of course, tends to call the judge's impartiality into question. Some judges in the Norwegian land consolidation system expressed their concern regarding playing an active role during mediation because their impartiality could be questioned. To avoid this, some judges - but not many - described their conduct as passive, particularly in cases were they felt that mediated settlements were unlikely. The more active judges informed the parties directly that their suggestions were an attempt to help the parties reach an agreement, which resolved the parties' disputes in more creative ways than a verdict allowed for. In a

Mediation in Land Consolidation and in Boundary Disputes 69

verdict, the judge has to make a decision based on the demands made by the parties. In mediation there is more freedom.

Wall and Rude (1989) divided mediation strategies into four groups of strategies: logical, aggressive, paternalistic, and client-oriented. Strategies from all four groups could be observed, but few involved aggressive tactics. In general judges used logical strategies. This is not a surprise given their considerable expertise in the issues at hand, and their dual role as judge and mediator. The more active judges, however, used aspects of paternalistic strategies when appropriate in specific situations. Mediation techniques used in the land consolidation court will be discussed briefly below.

Techniques observed in mediation of boundary disputes

Judges reported on the 35 different mediation techniques used. Nineteen of them were earlier identified by Schiller and Wall (1981) and are marked in Table 7.3 with an asterisk (*).

In a continuing education class on negotiation practices, 20 students were asked about the techniques. Nine of the students were land consolidation judges. The techniques marked with a cross (†) in Table 7.3 were found by the students to be unethical. Some of the techniques are specific to the nature of land disputes. These include mediation during the survey (No. 4), pointing out in the field where the proposed boundary will go (No. 6), arguing for a practical boundary as a solution (No. 11), and presenting the parties position on a map (No. 16). The other mediation techniques are of a more general nature. Some of the more controversial techniques for a judge to use (e.g. No. 24: talk to each party separately) were used only by few judges in very specific situations. Only the most active judges frequently used very settlement-oriented strategies where they proposed solutions (e.g. No. 31 and 32), and reminded the parties that a traditional trial verdict may not solve their problems (No. 23). The passive judges often did no more than raise the settlement issue (No. 19) and made no additional mediation efforts. In general, the judges spent much time on information sharing (e.g. No. 17), and on clarifying the nature of the dispute.

Mediation regarding the land consolidation plan

This is a different situation compared with the mediation of boundary disputes. The reallocation of land holdings is often an emotional process for the parties involved. An otherwise effective planning programme nevertheless results in conflict due to the tremendous personal and social changes resulting from land consolidation. Judges must take in to consideration the parties' different, and complex, relationships to the property in question (Goodale and Sky, 1998). Land consolidation planners frequently make the argument that the respective parties need time to get used to the 'new' arrangement. A land consolidation plan cannot

Methodologies, Models and Instruments

just be imposed from on high, without due consideration to these complex relationships. It is fundamentally important that the parties meaningfully contribute to the land consolidation planning process. Judges must never lose sight of the fact that the parties will be the ones using the land and living with the consequences of the new layout.

Table 7.3   Mediation techniques in boundary disputes

1	Asks questions or interview the parties.		
2	Brings in external issues.	†	
3	Reads the document (or the part of it) in which the parties have pleaded.		
4	Mediates during the survey.		
5	Starts to write the settlement agreement together with the parties.		
6	Point out in the field where the proposed boundaries will go.		
7	Outlines the factors that are important for the parties.		
8	Informs the parties what the verdict will be.	†	
9	Establishes a suitable environment for mediation and negotiation.		
10	Arranges a court session and mails out a settlement proposal to the parties.		
11	Argues for a practical boundary as a solution.		
12	Encourages the parties to settle.		
13	Encourages the parties to have meetings in groups.		
14	Tries to get the parties to see the case from the other's point of view.		
15	Invites the parties to think ahead.		
16	Outlines the parties' assertions in the form of a map, and then mediates.		
17	Informs the parties about facts.		*
18	Leaves the parties/clients together by themselves.		*
19	Raises the settlement issue, but nothing more assertive.		*
20	Channels discussion into areas, which have highest possibility of settlement.		*
21	Continues to bring up settlement during the case.	†	*
22	Informs the parties about missing facts or documents.		*
23	Reminds the parties that a verdict will not solve the problem.	†	*
24	Talks to each party separately about a settlement.	†	*
25	Reminds the parties about the high cost of going to trial.	†	*
26	Suggests settlement with or without asking for parties' input.	†	*
27	Suggests a specific settlement for the parties.		*
28	States what the case is worth for the parties.	†	*
29	Suggests parties split the difference.	†	*
30	Has one party pay the other party's costs.	†	*
31	Argues logically for concessions.		*
32	Offers alternative proposals not thought of by the parties.		*
33	Coerces or pressures parties to settle.	†	*
34	Requires settlement talks.	†	*
35	Tells the parties to concentrate on the relevant issues.		*

Mediation in Land Consolidation and in Boundary Disputes 71

The study indicates that in most cases, the judge or the land consolidation court was directly involved in planning. After a plenary court session with all the parties, several judges had informal meetings with one party or a group of parties. One judge, for example, organised meetings in the afternoon so the parties did not have to be away from work. Other judges did not recommend splitting up the parties during the case because they wanted all the parties to be able to hear what the others said to the judge. As can be seen from Table 7.4, the judges employed many different techniques. They also used a variety of methods for presenting a draft land consolidation plan. By using a GIS to make draft plans, the court was able to present a large number of alternative solutions. It must be emphasised that it is important that the parties contribute information early in the process, because the final result can then be more easily impacted.

Table 7.4   Mediation techniques in land consolidation planning

1	Presentation of several drafts after input from the parties.
2	Presentation of draft without input from the parties to show how land consolidation applies to the land tenure in the actual area.
3	Consensus over progress of the planning process and the making of time schedules.
4	Consensus over different planning methods, valuation methods, etc. (principles).
5	Emphasis on information about the planning process.
6	Talking with parties in groups or alone.
7	Establishing temporary regulations that could change during the planning process or during the course of land consolidation.
8	Motivating the parties to make suggestions.
9	Activating the parties by using 'sandwich paper' and maps to get input on layout of plots and holdings.
10	Using of preliminary oral proceedings.
11	Analysing the problems in the land consolidation field (area).
12	Analysing the parties' needs and relations to their property.
13	Zoning out elements that not will be subject to exchange.
14	Concentrating on the important issues.
15	Arranging informal meetings with one or more parties.
16	Negotiating with the owners of properties for sale in the land consolidation area.

The techniques used in land consolidation planning focus on the establishment of a consensus over the methods and progress in the planning process (No. 3 and 4). The judge often talks to the parties either in small groups or individuals (No. 6), or has informal meetings with the parties (No.15). Information gathering and sharing is emphasised in both boundary disputes and in planning. In land consolidation planning, the judges often motivate the parties to make suggestions and sketches (No. 8 and 9) and focus on making draft plans (No. 1 and 2). The methods used in land consolidation planning are considerably more active and solution-oriented than those employed in boundary disputes. The judge is also more involved with the parties in the process of developing plans. In summary, this short discussion is based on in depth interviews with judges and indicates that:

- a large set of mediation techniques are used;
- there are high variations between judges with regard to how active they are as judges;
- in general they mediate more actively and are more solution oriented in planning cases than in boundary disputes;
- their behaviour is affected by the presence of lawyers in the case;
- they find in general cases with few parties, low significance, uncertainty about rights and low conflict most suitable for mediation; and
- they are concerned with behavioural aspects of mediation when asked what is important for success.

Conclusion

The presented study of the Norwegian land consolidation courts confirms that mediation is an integral part of the judges' work on land issues. The judges mediate frequently and they intensify mediation when there are many parties, the size of land is significant, and when there is a high level of conflict. In particular, cases with joint ownership and/or investment were found to have a high level of controversy and mediation activities.

Mediation does not always lead to mediated settlements. However, even when final verdicts have to be made, the mediation process had positive results. Mediation through presentation and continuously redrafting of plans reduced the conflict level among the parties. Cases with mediated settlements had generally fewer parties, lower conflict levels, and were smaller than those decided through verdicts. In general, judges used more time mediating in cases that had the opposite characteristics. Therefore, it does not seem that judges discriminate in their mediation activity between cases based on their likelihood of achieving a mediated settlement. The reason may be that mediation has value in its own right (e.g. reducing conflicts). The results confirm the suggestion of Wall *et al.* (1984) that judges will mediate in most cases except for large simple cases. Mediated settlements, however, are achieved mostly in small and simple cases. Future research on mediation in land disputes should analyse in greater depth why mediators do not settle the more complex cases, and explore the characteristics of cases and mediation behaviour in the relatively few complex cases where settlements were reached.

The outcomes of the survey also indicate that there are considerable variations among judges both in preference for mediation and in techniques used in the mediation process. Some judges are extremely active and settlement oriented, especially in planning disputes. Other judges hardly mediate except for in the simplest cases. Several of the mediation techniques described by Schiller and Wall (1981) were found among Norwegian land consolidation judges. In addition, several techniques could be observed that are more specific to land disputes.

The study indicates that judges are in need of mediation training. The training need has become evident through the obtained results that show high behavioural variations between judges, and limited settlement success in more complex cases. The outcome of land consolidation process depends largely on the behaviour of the judge during the proceedings.

Acknowledgement

This study was supported by The Ministry of Agriculture in Norway.

References

Galanter, M., 1985. A settlement judge, not a trial judge: judicial mediation in the United States, *Journal of Law and Society*, **12**, 1-18.

Goodale, M.R. and Sky, P.K., 1998. Owners' relationships to property and land consolidation: a social approach, *Norwegian Journal of Mapping and Planning*, **58**, 264-268.

Kolb, D.M. and Associates, 1997. *When Talk Works. Profiles of Mediators*, Jossey-Bass Publishers, San Francisco.

Kovach, K.K., 1994. *Mediation: Principles and Practice*, West Publishing Co., St. Paul, Minnesota.

Kressel, K. and Pruitt, D.G., 1989. *Mediation Research. The Process and Effectiveness of Third-Party Intervention*, Jossey-Bass Publishers, San Francisco.

Moore, C.W., 1996. *The Mediation Process. Practical Strategies for Resolving Conflict* (2nd ed.), Jossey-Bass Publishers, San Francisco.

Pruitt, D.G. and Kressel, K., 1985. The mediation of social conflict, *Journal of Social Issues*, **41**(2), 1-10.

Rubino, R.G. and Jacobs, H.M., 1990. *Mediation and Negotiation for Planning, Land Use Management, and Environmental Protection: An Annotated Bibliography of Materials for the Period 1980-1989*, Council of Planning Librarians, Bibliography, No. 264.

Schiller, L.F. and Wall, H.L., 1981. Judicial settlement techniques, *The American Journal of Trial Advocacy*, **5**, 39-61.

Sevatdal, H., 1986. Land Consolidation in Norway. Unpublished paper, *Conference on Subdivision, Redesign and Neighborhood Pooling*, Fort Myers, Florida.

Shapiro, D., Drieghe, R. and Brett, J. (1985). Mediator behaviour and the outcome of mediation, *Journal of Social Issues*, **41**, 101-114.

Tomasic, R., 1980. *Mediation as an Alternative to Adjudication. Rhetoric and Reality in the Neighborhood Justice Movement*, Working Paper 1980:2, Disputes Processing Research Program, Law School, University of Wisconsin, 11-49.

Wall, J.A. and Rude, D.E., 1991. The judges as a mediator, *Journal of Applied Psychology*, **76**(1), 54-59.

Wall, J.A. and Rude, D.E., 1989. Judicial mediation of settlement negotiations. In: Kressel, K. and Pruitt, D.G. (eds.) *Mediation Research*, Jossey-Bass Publishers, San Francisco.

Wall, J.A., Rude, D.E. and Schiller, L., 1984. Judicial participation in settlement, *Missouri Journal of Dispute Resolution*, **1984**, 25-44.

Chapter 8

Policy Instruments in the Changing Context of Dutch Land Development

Daniëlle Groetelaers and Willem Korthals Altes

Introduction

Dutch municipalities have traditionally supplied land for development (Needham, 1992; Van der Krabben and Lambooy, 1993; Badcock, 1994; Van der Krabben, 1995; Needham and Verhage, 1998). Supplying land could typically involve a number of processes including draining it of water and raising it to well above the groundwater level, decontamination activities to clean up pollution, and providing services and associated infrastructure. This is very costly and takes time (Faludi and Korthals Altes, 1996). To achieve this, municipalities depend on central government assistance and grants, which are usually forthcoming. In the Netherlands there has been a general consensus between the tiers of government concerning spatial development (Needham, 1992; Faludi and Van der Valk, 1994). Dutch practice followed the 'golden rule' of development, that is, supplying the right amount of serviced land at the right location, at the right moment and at reasonable prices (Voß, 1997) and the supply of such land has been described as 'superbly efficient' (Mori, 1998). All this corresponds with the picture of the Netherlands as a planner's paradise (Faludi and Van der Valk, 1994). The consensus between the tiers of government, combined with government grants has, in many cases, guaranteed the implementation of spatial development plans. In this context, municipal land development companies have been seen as merely being implementation agencies (Kalt, 1998; Wigmans, 1998).

Nowadays this situation has changed. Several recent developments have tended to question the role of municipal land development companies in the Netherlands (Korthals Altes, 2000). Private agents are now able to purchase development land and municipalities no longer have a monopoly on land development. This forms a watershed in the context of the operation of municipal land agents, and has a large impact on the feasibility of the policy instruments used by municipalities. A recent survey amongst 180 Dutch municipalities (see also the research report written in Dutch by Groetelaers, 2000) gives an overview of the present state of policy instruments used for urban land development in extension areas throughout the Netherlands. This paper focuses on the present instrumental position of Dutch municipalities in the now rapidly changing context.

Towards the present context of accommodation

The situation is currently changing from a single-actor process controlled by local authorities to a multi-actor process, with various actors and various goals (Needham and Faludi, 1999). Both municipalities and landowners are now mutually dependent since the landowner or the organisation that has acquired the right to do so from the landowner can only implement land development. Private developers cannot develop without a municipal building permit, which has to been given either in accordance with the municipal land use plan (*bestemmingsplan*), or with a council decision, which has been approved by the province (the so-called Article 19 proceeding).

The housing programme (Figure 8.1) is now dominated by market sector housing (Dieleman, 1996) and private development companies are willing to invest in land to acquire development capacity. In many areas, they have been flexible to the new conditions and have acquired the land, whilst in a number of cases local municipalities have requested business connections to purchase land since the municipality was no longer prepared to acquire land.

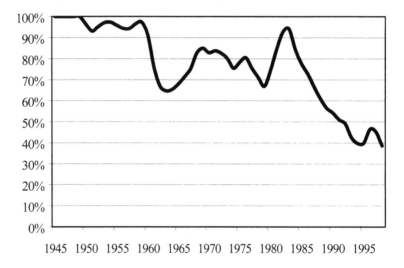

Figure 8.1   Share of state subsidised housing built in the Netherlands
Source: Central Bureau of Statistics (CBS), Maandstatistiek van de Bouwnijverheid, 1995-2000.

In responding to these changes, local government has requested judicial instruments that provide for better control of the land development process since the existing instruments of land development are unsuitable for a competitive development market. However, while central government is willing for local government to regulate the development of land, it is not prepared to grant it a monopoly over the process. On December 15th 2000, the Dutch Council of Ministers approved a National Land Policy Report (RVD, 2000) in which several instrumental innovations were introduced. These instruments are seen to represent important developments because:

- according to Voß (1997) the results of current Dutch land policy do not stem from the fine instruments of land policy, but from the municipal managerial skills. Municipalities are willing to take risks and invest in risky land development. They know how to bring actors together in the process. As such, they avoid impasses. There is for example, very little derelict land in Dutch cities (Wood, 1998). Municipalities purchase old industrial premises, often ahead of their relocation to more modern facilities, to start the redevelopment process;
- juridical instruments of the type set out in the Policy Report do not prescribe the actual processes. The instruments are part of a set of rules within which the processes take place. The Dutch are a society in which parties seek consensus (Faludi and Van der Valk, 1994) and this is also the case for private parties. It appears that development companies who have a consensual strategy towards local government and are willing to co-operate, have better results than companies who operate in a strategy of confrontation or in a strategy of ignorance. Major developing companies united in the NEPROM (the Dutch society of project developers) all follow a consensual strategy. They mainly attempt to come to an agreement with local government, sometimes by convincing local government that their own professional opinion is superior to the original municipal plan. Such an exchange of opinions may take some time in which parties might even loose confidence in the process itself. According to De Reus (1998) a director of a developing company, developers have two types of clients, i.e., the consumers of their products and the municipalities. This illustrates the strong position municipalities may have in the process. The actual position of local government may be much better, than the position resulting from the use of individual juridical instruments.

The changing situation in Dutch land policies (as set out in the recent National Land Policy Report) is subject of several research projects at the Department of Geodesy, Delft University of Technology. In this research, emphasis is placed on understanding the institutional position of the parties involved in the process. Thus, the research projects pay particular attention to the instruments of urban land development. The results of a questionnaire survey carried out to investigate the changing role of municipalities in the urban land development process are presented below (see also Groetelaers, 2000).

Start of the process

Figure 8.2 shows that at the beginning of the development process, most of the land is still owned by the original landowners.

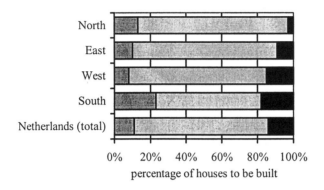

Figure 8.2   Land ownership at the start of the development process

At the start of the process, private developers, building companies, and investors had acquired a major part of the land (14%). In only a minority of the cases was this due to the owner holding a portfolio of agricultural land as a safe investment. The farmers themselves own most of the land and only one insurance company has a large agricultural land portfolio. The percentage of land owned by municipalities was slightly lower.

Figure 8.2 shows also that the tendency to acquire land early is stronger in the southern and western parts of the Netherlands, where there are more market opportunities due to higher house prices. Thus, municipalities fail to have a monopoly position, and both public and private parties compete in the land acquisition process.

Acquisition policy

It is commonly believed that an active acquisition policy is the best way for municipalities to react to the competing acquisitions by private developers (De Wolff, *et al.*, 2000). If municipalities wait until the last moment to purchase land, private parties will proceed faster. Land cannot be expropriated from landowners who are able and willing to implement the local land use plan (Overwater, 1999).

The survey shows that most municipalities share the idea of an active acquisition policy, with 47% of the municipalities in the urban extension areas using an active acquisition policy (Table 8.1). The survey also shows that 42% of the municipalities feel that land purchase is no longer necessary since the municipality already owns the land or there is a sound agreement with the original landowners. The remaining 11% of potential development area generates the greatest concern to the municipalities since it has been purchased by private developers or building companies that have not yet made sound agreements with the municipality. As urban extension areas differ in size, the percentages are also converted to percentages of the total number of planned dwellings (Table 8.1). This analysis shows that land acquisition is essentially no longer necessary in small areas since only 9% of the total dwellings are planned here. Municipalities are using an active acquisition policy for those areas in which 86% of the dwellings is projected. The municipalities can no longer purchase the land necessary for the remaining 5% of the dwellings.

Table 8.1   Acquisition policy of municipalities

	% extension areas	% dwellings
Active acquisition policy	47%	86%
Acquisition no longer necessary	42%	9%
Acquisition not possible	11%	5%

Table 8.2   Comparison of instruments which can be used to acquire land

	Agreement and/or negotiation	Pre-emption	Expropriation and/or Compulsory Purchase
Availability / applicability	can be used by all parties	can only be used by municipality	can only be used by municipality
Negotiations and acquisition	all actors are free to negotiate, acquisition when actors agree	Municipality has a right to negotiate (purchase) before others	municipality is obliged to negotiate, municipality is the only possible buyer
Opportunities for municipality	set in combination with pre-emption right or compulsory purchase	'back-up' for an active land policy (to prevent landowners selling to others)	can be used to push 'normal' negotiations
Threats for municipality	Can be used by all parties	Landowners can avoid a pre-emption right by developing themselves	landowners can avoid compulsory purchase by developing themselves

Dutch municipalities acquire land mostly by buying it, an instrument that can be used by every market party. However, municipalities have two additional instruments that enhance their position on the market (Table 8.2. See also De Haan *et al.*, 1996). The most radical instrument is expropriation by force of law (compulsory purchase), which enables municipalities to acquire land for housing or spatial development without the approval of the landowner, although the landowner

80 *Methodologies, Models and Instruments*

receives full financial compensation. Such an indemnification includes not only the market value of the land, but also may contain, for example, an extra amount of money to compensate reasonable loss suffered by the former owner. The other instrument is to exert legal priority rights (pre-emption right) on future urban extension areas (De Wolff, *et al.* 1998; 2000). If this is done, a landowner wishing to sell the land has to offer it initially to the municipality but is not, however, forced to sell the property. Almost a third of the Dutch municipalities have used a pre-emption right to acquire land since July 1996 (De Wolff, *et al.*, 2000). However, not all municipalities are allowed to use this instrument of which almost 50% have established a pre-emption right.

Based on the questionnaire, it appears that the municipalities have acquired approximately 74% of the land needed for urban land development. To acquire this land municipalities have used all the instruments identified in Table 8.2.

Municipalities have established a pre-emption right on almost all large (1,000 dwellings or more) urban extension areas (Table 8.3).

Table 8.3   Establishment of pre-emption rights

Pre-emption Right	Percentage of Areas	Percentage of Dwellings
Whole urban extension area	22%	62%
Part of the area	9%	19%
No pre-emption right	70%	19%

Expropriation is an instrument to directly acquire land but it can also be used indirectly to increase the pressure during negotiations, with the threat of expropriation helping a landowner decide to sell the property. Table 8.4 shows that expropriation proceedings are used in only 11% of the urban extension areas. This does not mean that 11% of the area is expropriated but that in parts of those areas expropriation may take place. Only 4% of the urban extension areas are actually expropriated. A municipality can only use expropriation if there is a land use plan (*bestemmingsplan*) associated with the urban extension under consideration.

Table 8.4 Existence of expropriation plans

Expropriation Plan	Percentage of Areas
Yes	11%
	(4 %: parts of areas actually expropriated)
Whole Area	1%
Part of the Area	10%
No	89%
Not Possible	4%
Not Necessary	63%
Not Yet	20%
Other Reason	2%

Co-operation and development approach

Municipalities do not necessarily have to acquire land to gain adequate control. In addition to the traditional model in which the municipality takes care of land development in total and sells building sites to the constructors, it is possible to distinguish three main models:

- exchange of land for building rights (public land development);
- joint public and private development; and
- private development (Levainen and Korthals Altes, 2000).

Exchange of land for building rights. In this model, municipalities still acquire the land and, in fact, developers and building companies are often willing to sell their land to the municipality (Needham, 1997). Their interest in the land is not primarily in making profit, but as a method of acquisition for building and project development. In exchange for the land, they receive money (often less than they acquired the land for) and the possibility of purchasing building sites after the municipality has provided the infrastructure. The private partner is often allowed to have some influence on the town plan of the area, although the municipality carries most of the financial risks of land development.

The survey gives insight into the nature of the building rights involved in the 'exchange model' (Table 8.5). In cases where agreements exist on land prices and there is an obligation to buy, the risks associated with the buying and selling of land are transferred from the municipality to the developer.

82   *Methodologies, Models and Instruments*

Table 8.5   Supplementary agreements with building rights

Agreements	Percentage of Building Rights
Site within location were building may take place	66%
Land prices	63%
Obligation to buy	56%
Right to be consulted in planning process	41%
Others	34%
No supplementary agreements	6%

Joint public and private development. In this model the municipality and one or more private companies, contribute land to a joint public-private company. A company composed of the municipality and private parties, shares the risks and the management of the area. The share of the municipality differs. In the development area of Leidschenveen (7,000 dwellings and 270,000m^2 of commercial development, near The Hague) the share of the municipality of Leidschendam is 30%. In other areas, the municipal share is often 50%.

Private development (concession). In this model, the municipality makes agreements about costs for infrastructure provision. The development company often provides the infrastructure within the plan (the primary infrastructure), and the municipality makes a contribution towards the secondary infrastructure outside the plan. Unlike the other models, the municipality shares no market risk in this model. The agreement includes the stipulations between the private and the public partners, with the private partner taking the risks.

Combination of models. Sometimes combinations of models are used. In IJburg (near Amsterdam), and Ypenburg (near The Hague) the municipality is responsible for the main infrastructure of the area. The municipality develops the main roads, major parks, and water works. In the integral development, a part of the planned area (say sites for 500 dwellings) is transferred to the private parties. The programme and the recovery of costs for the main infrastructure are regulated in the agreements.

The use of the models. Most municipalities still prefer public development, which is often achieved through the exchange of rights (see Table 8.6). Municipalities place a great effort in acquiring land. The percentage of 'public development' is even higher when converted to the number of dwellings to be built (difference in size of the areas). It seems that municipalities in particular are willing to control the land development process in larger areas, in order to create an integral and diverse development. It is interesting to note also that private involvement in larger areas

Policy Instruments in the Changing Dutch Context

often lies in public-private partnerships (joint development), whereas in many smaller areas private companies work in concession.

Table 8.6   Development approach

Development Approach	Percentage of Areas	Percentage of Dwellings
Public development	58%	68%
Public-private partnership	9%	22%
Private development	15%	5%
Combination	6%	2%
Not yet decided	11%	2%

It is noticeable that only 11% of the urban extension area municipalities (2% of the dwellings to be built) say that they do not yet know what development approach they will follow. As these figures arise from choices made by municipalities, it is interesting to compare the percentages with land ownership at the beginning of the development process (Table 8.7). Private parties own more land in areas where private development will take place than in areas where public development is going to occur.

Table 8.7   Land ownership at the start and development approach

	Municipality	Original Landowners	Private Parties
Public development	14%	76%	10%
Public-private partnership	1%	74%	25%
Private development	14%	55%	31%
Combination	12%	86%	2%

There are four stages of involvement by public and private parties during the different stages of land development. These are land acquisition, temporary control of the acquired land, supplying the land, and the actual physical changes. Every stage comprises the execution of a task and taking the risks for it. In each stage, approximately 50% of the tasks are taken by the municipality alone (Figure 8.3), with a smaller part (approximately 15% to 25%) being the mutual responsibility of the municipality and private actors.

84   *Methodologies, Models and Instruments*

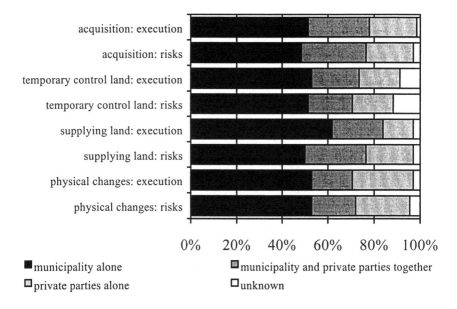

Figure 8.3   Involvement of public and private actors during the different stages of land development

Evaluation by municipalities

The questionnaire asked municipalities to evaluate their own instrumental position by describing three 'bottlenecks' encountered throughout the land development process (see Table 8.8). The responses identified that municipalities consider land acquisition to be the most important bottleneck. Owning the land increases the influence on the urban land development process. The second most important bottleneck the view of municipalities is recovering the costs for infrastructure provision when the land cannot be acquired. Previously, when local authorities were completely in control of the urban land development process (i.e. they owned all the land), all costs could be recovered.

Table 8.8   Bottlenecks perceived by municipalities

Stage	Main Bottlenecks
Initiating / Planning	Establishing ambitions
Changing land use plan	Procedures (complexity and time span)
	Co-operation with private developers
Land acquisition	Acquisition (general)
	Acquisition (other parties are first)
	Failings in Pre-emption Law
	Self-realisation by other parties
	Increasing price level
	Co-operation with private developers
Physical changes	
Financing / costs	Recovering costs

Conclusions

The results of the survey do not give any basis for the assumption of a complete breakdown of the Dutch system of land development (Verhage and Needham, 1997). Dutch municipalities, in a large majority of cases, are able to gain satisfactory control over the land development process, through using their land management skills, within a context defined by, amongst other factors, their instrumental position (Faludi and Van der Valk, 1994; Needham, 1992; Voß, 1997).

The instruments in use are also still strong enough for municipalities to gain a central position in the land development process. However, discussions and research on instruments for urban land development often fail to focus on the actual use of instruments within a complex set of multiple actors. The emphasis often lies in the theoretical juridical achievements of a single instrument in a worst-case scenario. Within such a view there are many deficiencies and gaps in instruments for urban land development. However, it is not proven that in practise that these failures of individual instruments have severe negative consequences. The survey may even lead to an opposite conclusion. It is, therefore, remarkable that so little attention is paid to the principle that it may be possible to obtain better results in urban land development, through using existing instruments in different ways. At the present, local government is generally able to ensure that development takes place in a well-concerted and orderly way. It is usually possible to develop the quality that local government strives for in such a way that development pays for the provision of the infrastructure.

Of course, a large-scale review of the instruments, as announced by Dutch government (RVD, 2000), might improve processes. These proposed changes include an exploitation permit, changes in pre-emption law, the taxation of building

86   *Methodologies, Models and Instruments*

on farmland and other open areas, and a set of laws making the participation of citizens in the land development process obligatory. Further research into these matters will provide a deeper insight in the qualities of Dutch instruments for land development. It will also make it possible to formulate better-founded proposals for the improvements of land policy instruments and their use.

References

Badcock, B., 1994. The strategic implication for the Randstad of the Dutch property system, *Urban Studies*, **31**(3), 425-445.

CBS, 1995-2000. *Maandstatistiek van de Bouwnijverheid*, Heerlen.

Cronbach, L.J., Ambron, S.R., Dornbusch, S.M., Hess, R.D., Hornik, R.C., Phillips, D.C., Walker, D.F. and Weiner, S.S., 1980. *Toward Reform of Program Evaluation: Aims, Methods, and Institutional Arrangements*, Jossey-Bass, San Francisco/London.

Dieleman, F., 1996. The quiet revolution in Dutch housing policy, *TESG*, **87**(3), 275-282.

Faludi, A. and Korthals Altes, W.K., 1994. Evaluating communicative planning: a revised design for performance research, *European Planning Studies*, **2**(4), 403-418.

Faludi, A., and Korthals Altes, W.K., 1996. Marketing planning and its dangers: how the new housing crisis in the Netherlands came about, *Town Planning Review*, **67**(2), 183-202.

Faludi, A. and van der Valk, A.J., 1994. *Rule and Order: Dutch Planning Doctrine in the Twentieth Century*, Kluwer Academic Publishers, Dordrecht.

Groetelaers, D.A., 2000. *Instrumentarium Locatieontwikkeling: Nederlandse Praktijk*, Delft University Press, Delft.

Haan, P., de, Drupsteen, Th. G. and Fernhout, R., 1996. *Bestuursrecht in de Sociale Rechtsstaat, Deel 1: Ontwikkeling, Organisatie en Instrumentarium*, Kluwer, Deventer.

Kalt, N., 1998. De regie bij het realiseren van ruimtelijk beleid. In: Blitz E., et al, *De Stad: de Spelers, de Meters, de Stuurders*, Elsevier Bedrijfsinformatie, Den Haag, 97-107.

Keers, G.P., Terbrack, C. and Knegt, F.R., 1988. *Grondprijzen voor de Gesubsidieerde Woningbouw*, TK 1987-1988, 19623, 34 Staatsuitgeverij, Den Haag.

Keers, G.P., 1989. *Het Rijksgrondbeleid voor de Woningbouw Sinds 1900: een Historisch Onderzoek*, Ministerie van Volkshuisvesting, Ruimtelijke Ordening en Milieubeheer, Den Haag.

Kolpron Consultants, 2000. *Kostenverhaal in de Grondexploitatie op VINEX-Locaties*, Neprom, Voorburg.

Korthals Altes, W.K., 2000. Economic forces and Dutch strategic planning. In: Salet, W. and Faludi, A. (eds.) *The Revival of Strategic Spatial Planning*, KNAW Verhandelingen, Afd. Letterkundige Nieuwe Reeks 181, Royal Netherlands Academy of Sciences, Amsterdam, 67-78.

Krabben, E., van der, 1995. *Urban dynamics: A Real Estate Perspective: An Institutional Analysis of the Production of the Build Environment*, Amsterdam (Thesis).

Krabben, E., van der and Lambooy, J.G., 1993. A theoretical framework for the functioning of the Dutch property market, *Urban Studies*, **30**(8), 1381-1397.

Levainen, K.I. and Korthals Altes, W.K. 2000. The public-private co-operation in land development: a comparative study in Finland and in the Netherlands, Paper for the RICS conference *The Cutting Edge*, London.

Mori H., 1998. Land conversion at the urban fringe: a comparative study of Japan, Britain and the Netherlands, *Urban Studies*, **35**(9), 1541-1558.

Needham, B., 1992. A theory of land prices when land is supplied publicly, *Urban Studies*, **29**, 669-681.

Needham, B., 1997. Land policy in the Netherlands, *TESG*, **88**(3), 291-296.

Needham, B. and Faludi, A., 1999. Dutch growth management in a changing market, *Planning, Practice and Research*, **14**(4), 481-491.

Needham, B. and Verhage, R., 1998. The effects of land policy: quantity as well as quality is important, *Urban Studies*, **35**(1), 25-44.

Overwater, P.S.A., 1999. Onteigening en een beroep op zelfrealisatie binnen het kader van een nieuw, sturend gemeentelijk grondbeleid, *Agrarisch Recht*, **59**(12), 631-644.

Reus, C.E.C., de, 1998. Vastgoedontwikkelaars moeten over smaak twisten, *Architectuur Lokaal*, Oktober 1998 (**21**), 5-6.

RVD, 2000. *Nota Grondbeleid Vastgesteld*, Persbericht Ministerraad, 15 December 2000, Rijksvoorlichtingsdienst, Den Haag.

Schmidt-Eichstaedt, G., 1999. Baulandbereitstellung nach dem niederländischen Modell, *Grundstücksmarkt und Grundstückswert*, **10**(2), 65-72.

Slangen, L.H.G. and Polman, N.B.P., 1997. Waarde van grond: bied-en koopprijzen 1963-1994, *Agrarisch Recht*, **57**(11), 524-545.

Verhage, R. and Needham, B., 1997. Negotiating about the residential environment: it is not only money that matters, *Urban Studies*, **34**(12), 2053-2068.

Voß, W., 1997. Niederlande, In: Dieterich, B. and Dieterich, H., (eds.), *Boden - Wem Nutzt er? Wen Stützt er? Neue Perspektiven des Bodenrechts*, Bauwelt Fundamente 119, Vieweg, Braunschweig/Wiesbaden, 109-123.

Wigmans, G., 1998. *De Facilitaire Stad: Rotterdams Grondbeleid en Postmodernisering*, Delft University Press, Delft.

Wolff, H.W., de, Greef, J.H., de, Groetelaers, D.A., Jong, J. de and Korthals Altes, W.K., 2000. *Gebruik en Effecten Wet Voorkeursrecht Gemeenten*, Delft University Press, Delft.

Wolff, H.W., de, Groetelaers, D.A. and Jong, J., de, 1998. *Eerste Ervaringen met de Gewijzigde Wet Voorkeursrecht Gemeenten*, Delft University Press, Delft.

Wood, B., 1998. *Vacant Land in Europe*, Lincoln Institute of Land Policy Working Paper, WP98BW1, Lincoln Institute of Land Policy, Cambridge.

Chapter 9

Modelling the Development of Sustainable Communities in Edinburgh's South East Wedge

Mark Deakin

Introduction

The on-going review of structure plans in the United Kingdom has highlighted the attractiveness of new settlements as an alternative to cramming, peripheral expansion and urban sprawl. This paper examines the argument for new settlements appearing in the Written Statement on Lothian's 1994 Structure Plan Review (Lothian Regional Council, 1994). It goes on to establish how the experiments going on in Edinburgh's South East Wedge are transforming the new settlement phenomenon in to the search for a plan-led, environmentally friendly and sustainable pattern of settlement. It draws attention to the Interim Development Framework put in place to support the plan-led, environmentally friendly experiment and settlement model adopted for such purposes. After making a number of observations on the development of sustainable communities in Edinburgh's South East Wedge, the paper draws some conclusions on the nature of the experiment.

The Written Statement

The 1994 Written Statement on the Lothian Structure Plan Review states that:

> the development of Edinburgh can no longer be accommodated within the existing boundaries of the City ... cramming of development in brown field sites is no longer an option for Edinburgh.

Neither is development by peripheral expansion around the edge of the City's greenbelt. There are:

> simply not enough brown field sites to develop in Edinburgh and peripheral expansion around the edge of the City would put too much pressure on the greenbelt and result in urban sprawl.

Modelling the Development of Sustainable Communities 89

The solution, the statement suggests, rests with the development of new settlements. In particular with the:

> development of new settlements on a 1,600 hectare site at the periphery of Edinburgh and in an area of the City's greenbelt known as the South East Wedge.

As an exercise in the management of growth, the statement suggests that plan-led experiments of this kind can protect the environment and the proposal to:

> develop new settlements in the South East Wedge of Edinburgh provides the City with just such an opportunity.

The reasons put forward to explain why the development provides such an opportunity are as follow:

- representing less than 10% of the greenbelt, the site has the capacity to accommodate 35% of Edinburgh's land use requirements, 60% of the City's population growth, 15% of additional households and 30% of future employment opportunities;
- the site has the capacity to carry such a level of growth due to spare capacity in both the utility and transportation networks and because it is already well serviced with out-of-town shopping centres, retail and warehouse parks, leisure and entertainment facilities; and
- in releasing pressure for speculative development around the edge of the City and protecting the greenbelt, the site provides the opportunity for Edinburgh to make sure the use of land, utilities, transportation networks and both retail and leisure services, is environmentally friendly and fosters a more sustainable pattern of settlement.

The case the Written Statement makes for the development of new settlements is compelling. It goes a long way to illustrate the strategic significance of the 1,600 hectare site in Edinburgh's South East Wedge. It suggests the South East Wedge offers Edinburgh an alternative to the speculative development of green field sites, the peripheral expansion that follows and urban sprawl, which this produces. Why? Because it is seen to provide the opportunity for Edinburgh to plan the City's expansion into the greenbelt and protect the environment through the pattern of settlement it develops for such purposes.

The new settlement phenomenon

The development of such settlements is, of course, not as new a phenomenon as the title would suggest. As Ward (1992) establishes, with the privatisation of the New

90 *Methodologies, Models and Instruments*

Towns Commission, private consortiums have sought to develop new settlements as an alternative to peripheral expansion and urban sprawl. It is a phenomenon that Glasson *et al.* (1994) also examines. Their research show that during the review of structure plans carried out between 1988-93, 46 new settlement proposals had been submitted to planning authorities throughout the UK yet only two developments were successful in receiving outline planning consent. As Ratcliff and Stubbs (1996) also noted the tight fiscal regime local governments operated under during this period. This made the development of new settlements by private consortiums attractive, although they were too speculative, not supported by the planning system, and unable to allay any fears the public had about their impact on the environment.

It is noticeable that the proposal to develop new settlements in Edinburgh's South East Wedge goes a long way to avoid the difficulties experienced by many of its predecessors. It is not only supported by a written statement but proposes to be plan-led and environmentally friendly. While going a long way to distinguish the development of new settlements in Edinburgh from previous experiments of this type, it is not these qualities that mark it out from its predecessors. As a more advanced experiment in the modelling of alternatives to peripheral expansion and urban sprawl, the qualities that distinguish the proposal to develop new settlements in the South East Wedge from its predecessors are to be found elsewhere. It is the proposal to develop a sustainable pattern of settlement, which distinguishes the experiment going on in Edinburgh from its predecessors. This is because the object is not the development of new settlements *per se*, but that of an environmentally friendly, sustainable pattern of settlement.

Towards sustainable settlement patterns

The shift in emphasis from new settlements towards the development of environmentally friendly sustainable settlement patterns does have a purpose. It is to highlight how the experiments taking place in Edinburgh are transforming the new settlement phenomenon. What it illustrates is that the new settlement phenomenon is no longer about the speculative development of green field sites the transformation of those sites into an experiment concerning the management of growth in the green belt, which is plan-led, environmentally friendly, and produces a sustainable pattern of settlement. This is also important because it identifies the plan-led, environmentally friendly pattern of settlement and advances a settlement pattern, which is sustainable in the sense that it provides an alternative to peripheral expansion and urban sprawl.

The interim development framework

The search for a pattern of settlement that is sustainable was addressed by the 1996 Interim Development Framework (IDF) (Chesterton, 1996). Here, attention is directed towards their design, which has a distinctive urban culture, spatially compact form, and is able to develop as a set of sustainable communities. The question is how in turn to use the development as a means of modelling an environmentally friendly settlement pattern, which represents an alternative to peripheral expansion around the edge of the City and urban sprawl this produces? The settlement model, which is proposed in the document as the framework for the development of the South East Wedge addresses these two questions.

The settlement model is based upon how the IDF makes use of and draws upon the Department of the Environment's (DoE's) Planning Research Programme. In particular, it addresses the studies of:

- growth and the green belt (DoE, 1993a);
- alternative settlement patterns (Breheny *et al.*, 1993); and the
- infrastructure service provision (transport in particular) report prepared by the DoE (1993b).

In England and Wales, the research programme provides the basis for the Planning Guidance Notes (PGNs) whilst in Scotland these notes appear in the form of the National Planning Policy Guidelines (NPPGs). The research in Scotland provides the basis for the following:

- NPPG1 (The Planning System) and its policy guidance on growth management, green belts, environmental protection and the development of sustainable settlement patterns;
- use of NPPG1 to ensure that such a plan-led development is environmentally friendly in the sense which it is consistent *with This Common Inheritance* (HM Government, 1990,1991, 1994a);
- incorporation of statements made concerning environmental planning in *Sustainable Development: The UK Strategy* (HM Government, 1994b) into such plan-led developments;
- adoption of these into the on-going review of structure plans;
- use of strategic environmental assessment to ensure policies on growth management and the use of green belts to protect the environment, are consistent with those documents (DoE, 1991; 1993c); and
- use of the DoE's (1993c) *Environmental Appraisal of Development Plans*, to carry out such assessments and provide statements on growth management, use of the green belt, and protection of the environment.

92 *Methodologies, Models and Instruments*

Drawing upon this plan-led and environmentally friendly framework for the development of sustainable communities in Edinburgh's South East Wedge, the IDF document goes on to outline the settlement model which it propose should be adopted for such purposes.

The settlement model

The settlement model proposed in the document as a design solution appears under the heading of 'sustainable communities'. Under this heading, attention is drawn to the principles of sustainable development, which the document argues such settlements should be based upon. Modelling the development of sustainable communities, the document proposes that Edinburgh's experiment in managing growth through plan-led, environmentally friendly settlement patterns should be based on a:

- distinctive urban culture;
- spatially compact form;
- strong landscape framework in a countryside setting;
- set of neighbourhoods;
- high density of population;
- balance of land use, economic and social structures;
- energy conscious public transportation network;
- high level of infrastructure and shared service provision;
- pattern of settlement that is able to integrate existing communities with those emerging from the development; and
- financial structure that is viable in the short, medium, and long term future.

These qualities reflect the studies of alternative settlement patterns by Breheny (1992a; 1992b), Breheny and Rookwood (1993), and Breheny *et al.*, (1993).

Developing sustainable communities

The proposal to develop a distinctive urban culture is defined in terms of what it represents as an alternative settlement model, which represents an alternative to the suburban lifestyle. The suburban lifestyle, whose particular brand of resource intensive consumerism expands into the periphery and demands the speculative development of green field sites around the edge of the City. This, in turn, requires local authorities to release land from the greenbelt and, as experience suggests, leads to the coalescence of settlements around the edge of the city resulting in a loss of identity and the break up of communities under the process of urban sprawl.

Modelling the Development of Sustainable Communities　　　93

The model proposed suggests that the City needs to manage growth in a way that is plan-led, environmentally friendly, and which produces a distinctive urban culture for the spatially compact forms of settlement it proposes to develop. Drawing on the experiences of alternative settlements throughout the UK, the IDF document suggests that if alternatives to peripheral expansion and urban sprawl are to produce settlement patterns, which develop as sustainable communities, they should have:

- distinctive urban characters;
- spatially compact forms;
- strong landscape frameworks in county side settings;
- relatively high population densities;
- mixed land uses;
- balanced economic and social structures; and
- provide energy conscious public transportation systems (see Breheny, 1995; Selman 1996; Brown, 1998).

Hall and Ward (1998) study the other qualities listed in the IDF:

- high levels of infrastructure;
- shared service provision;
- pattern of settlement that is able to integrate existing communities with those emerging from the development; and
- have a financial structure, which is viable in the short, medium and long term horizon.

In this study, the development of such settlements in the Thames Corridor, and the cities of Cambridge and Peterborough are considered. Particular attention is drawn to the integrative qualities of such settlements and tight fiscal regime under which they operate for the development of such settlements requires a number of disclosures to be made about their financial viability (Hall and Ward, 1998).

Sustainable communities in Edinburgh's South East Wedge

In Edinburgh, this alternative to suburban culture is derived from the decision to restrict development around the edge of the City and to concentrate it on a 1,600 hectare, green field site known as the South East Wedge (see Figure 9.1). This particular process of peripheral expansion is to be planned rather than being market-led. Furthermore, the settlement pattern will be environmentally friendly in the sense that it will have a distinctive urban culture, take on a spatially compact form, and will not result in any coalescence, loss of identity, and break-up of communities in this part of the City's greenbelt. The strong landscape framework

94   *Methodologies, Models and Instruments*

and countryside setting, which the model proposes guards against the possibility of any such coalescence. It proposes that the development should make use of natural features, woodlands, and country parks as a way of separating the peripheral housing estate from the existing former mining village, which the model proposes should form the focus of the development (see Figure 9.2).

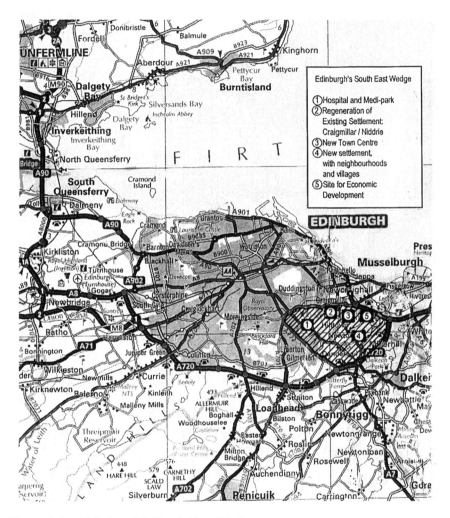

Figure 9.1   Edinburgh's South East Wedge
Source: Lothian Regional Council (1994)

The possibility of peripheral expansion is discounted through the measures proposed by the model for the communities in question. This is because the peripheral housing estate will be subjected to an urban regeneration programme and a limited town centre expansion scheme advocated for the former mining village. The physical separation of the existing settlement from the new development is also a major theme for the rest of the site. The 3 new settlements should be capable of accommodating up to 20,000 people. Although 'clustered' around each other, the model suggests that the 5,000 additional households forming the development should be physically separated from one another as neighbourhoods. The population density of these settlements is forecast to be between 50-200 per hectare and, to compensate for this, it is proposed that these neighbourhoods should have a balanced set of land uses. This will include residential, commercial (light industrial, business, warehouse and distribution, and retail) use, and communal services (transportation, recreational, education, and health). The design also allows for the neighbourhood units to have a balanced (low, middle, and upper income) economic and social structure (see Figure 9.2).

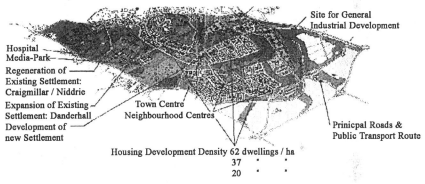

Figure 9.2 The settlement model
Source: Chesterton (1996)

Living and working environment

In the interests of providing a 'high quality working and living environment', the model allows for the development of an energy conscious transportation system. It should incorporate a number of measures, for example, including a public transport corridor, bus priority proposal, park and ride system, and traffic-calming scheme. It also suggests that some of the neighbourhoods should be car free and that residents should be within easy walking distance of public transport facilities.

Infrastructure requirements

These include land consolidation works, sites, and service provision, transportation, recreation, education, and health provision. In view of this, the model proposes that the transportation, recreation, education, and health services should be shared between the peripheral housing estate, former mining village and neighbourhoods forming the settlement pattern proposed for the development of sustainable communities. The neighbourhoods emerging from the development will not be able to provide either the employment, recreational, education, health or retail services needed to support the high quality working and living environment the model suggests is needed for the development of sustainable communities. This is the key factor in the integration of the peripheral housing estate, the former mining village, and neighbourhoods into a sustainable settlement pattern. The regenerated peripheral housing estate, expanded former mining village, and neighbourhoods will have access to, and share and co-operate in providing the infrastructures and services needed for the high quality living and working environments forming the settlement pattern. This will prevent the coalescence, loss of identity and break up of communities resulting from this process of peripheral expansion.

Financial viability

The financial viability issue tackles particular difficulties associated with the geology of the site and high level of infrastructure and service provision needed to develop the settlement pattern. Given the abnormal preparation costs, high infrastructure, and service content, the framework sets out the yield of the development in the form of land receipts. The cash flows are analysed over the short, medium and long-term horizons and discounted at the opportunity cost of capital. The income is based on the sale of mixed land use sites (residential, light industrial and retail) and represents the development value of the sites with planning permission. The costs include the purchase of land at existing use value (i.e., without the development proposal) and the capital expenditure on the infrastructures required to service the sites. The existing use value is taken to represent the sum of agricultural and 'hope value'. The capital expenditure represents the cost of site preparation, providing the recreation, education, health, and public transportation network. The discounted cash flow analysis supporting the appraisal illustrates that the project should yield an 11% internal rate of return (i.e. surplus of income over cost of development).

As a development appraisal, the exercise follows the guidelines set out in the DOEs (1991) publication on *Policy Appraisal and the Environment*. It also makes use of DOEs (1993d) document *on Making Markets Work for the Environment* and the Local Government Management Board's publication (LGMB, 1994) on *Greening Economic Development*. Based upon these publications, a number of economic instruments can be used to establish the financial viability of the project. These include for example, cash flow analysis, discounting procedures and cost benefit analysis techniques. From this, it is

Modelling the Development of Sustainable Communities

possible to establish whether the quality of the working and living environments making up the development produce enough planning gain for the land market to fund the infrastructure services upon which the settlement pattern is based and the sustainable communities are seen to rest.

Some observations

It is evident the growth management strategy adopted for Edinburgh's South East Wedge is clearly plan-led. The development of green field sites need not be speculative, but can be plan-led and this in turn provides the opportunity for such experiments to be environmentally friendly. This is because the distinct urban culture of the spatially-compact forms proposed as a design solution, provides a settlement pattern which protects the green belt, guards against coalescence, loss of identity and any possible break up of communities resulting from the subsequent pressure for infill development.

It should perhaps also be noted that it is difficult to establish the degree to which this experiment can be said to be environmentally friendly. Whether it is environmentally friendly or merely an attempt to 'green economic development' is perhaps the important question. Some observers of the new settlement phenomenon suggest that such experiments are environmentally friendly whilst others see them as little more than an attempt to 'gloss over' such issues and green economic development (see, Selman, 1996; and Davoudi, 1997, respectively, for a representation of such positions). As Gibbs *et al.* (1996) point out, whatever position is taken on the issue, it is a matter that raises questions about the integration of the environmental and economics in the development of sustainable communities. Given that the experiment in the South East Wedge of Edinburgh proposes to provide a model for managing growth that is not only plan-led and environmentally friendly, but offers a design solution that is also efficient in greening economic development, the question of integration is one of particular significance.

The environmentally friendly nature

The immediate difficulties faced in trying to establish the development's environmentally friendly nature, rest with the effective absence of the data needed for such an assessment. This is because:

- despite drawing upon the DOEs Planning Research Programme and using NPPG1 to guide the on-going review of the structure plan, strategic environmental assessments, and appraisals of how to manage growth, the IDF document provides very little evidence to support the claim that the plan-led development produces an environmentally friendly settlement pattern;

98 *Methodologies, Models and Instruments*

- while placing a great deal of emphasis on the capacity, the site has to carry a distinctive urban culture in spatially compact forms, set within strong landscape frameworks and countryside settings, the model and design solution, it proposes no formal assessment of its ecological footprint, bio-diversity, or natural capital.

In its current form the model and design solution is vulnerable to many of the criticisms Glasson *et al.* (1994) and Ratcliff and Stubbs (1996), have previously made about the new settlement phenomena, together with the sometimes less than friendly way that plan-led developments of this kind treat the environment. Lichfield (1996) also echoes these criticisms. This suggests that little has been learnt about the environmental values of the urban culture, spatially compact forms, strong landscape framework, and countryside setting that the model sets out, or how in turn this leads to a position where the design of the neighbourhoods, population densities, socio-economic structures, energy conscious public transport, high levels of both infrastructure and service provision, produce an efficient greening of economic development. An efficient greening of economic development that is financially viable and may be taken to represent an environmentally friendly pattern of settlement for the development of sustainable communities (also see, Beatley, 1995; Campbell, 1996; Cosgriff and Steinmann, 1998).

Little more than an aesthetic?

Set against the critique of such models and the design solutions they advance, the environmentally friendly nature of the settlement pattern might be seen to add up to little more than an aesthetic that reduces the environmental value of ecologically sound designs to the distinctive urban culture, spatially compact forms, strong landscape framework, and countryside setting that the model sets out. Furthermore, it is concerned with the design of neighbourhoods, population densities, land uses, socio-economic structures, and public transportation systems that form the infrastructures required to service high quality living and working environments. These are perceived to be friendly because the land market upon which they rest produce sufficient planning gain to efficiently green the economic development of the peripheral housing estate, former mining village, and neighbourhoods making it financially viable to produce an environmentally friendly pattern of settlement. An environmentally friendly pattern of settlement is sustainable in the sense that it is perceived to guard the communities being developed against everything seen as a possible threat to them in the form of the coalescence of settlements, loss of identity, and break-up of communities that results from the pressure for infill development traditionally associated with peripheral expansion of this kind.

Its value, limitations, and short-fallings

The value of the aesthetic may be seen to lie with its suggestion that it is possible for the model to design high quality living and working environments, which are

Modelling the Development of Sustainable Communities 99

friendly because the land market upon which they rest produces enough planning gain to efficiently green the economic development in question and make it financially viable. Thus, the economic development of the regeneration programme, town centre expansion, and new neighbourhoods makes it financially viable and, in turn, produces an environmentally friendly pattern of settlement.

If this is where the value of the aesthetic lies and it certainly appears to be, then its limitations and short-fallings need to be recognised. In its current form the model is unable to tell us whether the design of the high quality living and working environments, which it advances, are ecologically sound. Whether or not the high quality living and working environments are friendly because they are ecologically sound, or the land market produces enough planning gain to efficiently green the economic development of the estate, village and neighbourhoods to make it financially viable, exposes the limitations of the model and proposed design solution. In its current form, the model can only address one question and not the other.

Ecologically sound and efficient?

The question is perhaps, whether it is an answer to the former or latter, which has the right to make claims about the environmentally friendly nature of the settlement pattern? With the former - even though the model does not raise them - the questions are to do with the site's ecological footprint, bio-diversity, and environmental loading and are concerned with environmental values and matters. It relates to the levels of energy consumption, biomass, waste and emissions, and whether those levels produce high quality living and working environments that are friendly because they are ecologically sound. They are matters to do with the ecology of the distinctive urban cultures, spatially compact forms, strong landscape frameworks, and countryside settings, and whether the urban cultures are ecologically sound. This provides an appropriate basis for the population densities, land uses, socio-economic structures and public transportation systems that form the infrastructures, which are required to service the high quality living and working environments. The latter question is concerned with the land market and level of planning gain needed to be efficient in greening economic development, and the levels needed to efficiently green the economic development and make it a financial viability.

The question of integration

The question that arises is to what extent ecologically sound or ecologically efficient can be relied upon to produce an environmentally friendly pattern of settlement? The former deals with environmental values and matters concerning energy consumption, biomass, waste and emissions, whilst the latter is concerned only with land markets and the levels of planning gain needed to efficiently green economic development and make it financially viable (Deakin, 1996; 1997; 1999a; 1999b). Viewed in this way, the former concerns have to be seen as keys when searching for an answer to whether the high quality living and working

100   *Methodologies, Models and Instruments*

environments are friendly. Whether the environments are friendly because they are ecologically sound, or if the land markets and levels of planning gain efficiently green the economic development and make it financially viable. If such concerns about energy consumption, biomass, waste and emissions are seen to be key, then it shows that there is a pressing need for these matters to be integrated into such models. It also illustrates there is a critical requirement for the designs which follow to demonstrate whether they are ecologically sound. Whether they are ecologically sound and because of this, use land markets and levels of planning gain, they produce in a manner that is not only efficient in greening economic development, but which also has the consequence of making it financially viable (Deakin, 2000; 2002).

These needs and requirements are both pressing because as soon as we draw a critical distinction between the environmental values of ecologically sound designs and the land markets required to produce levels of planning gain, green economic development and make it financially viable, questions arise about:

- the science and technologies needed to make the energy consumption, biomass, waste and emissions of the high quality living and working environments friendly;
- how those technologies provide the infrastructures required for the high quality living and working environments to be friendly because they are ecologically sound;
- the degree to which it is the science and technologies of the infrastructures and ecologically sound designs, rather than articulation of the said land markets and planning gain, that efficiently greens economic development and makes it financially viable;
- how the science, technologies, infrastructures and ecologically sound designs in turn use the said market and levels of planning gain to efficiently green economic development and make it financially viable; and
- how this particular, ecologically sound use of the land markets and planning gain provides an efficient greening of economic development, makes it financially viable and produces environmentally friendly settlement patterns which are sustainable.

Against the science and technology of ecologically-sound designs, it can be seen that matters concerning the articulation of land markets and planning gain tell us little concerning the real issues associated with the transformation of the new settlement phenomenon, i.e., with design solutions, which are valued because they are ecologically sound. With ecologically sound design solutions, their high quality living and working environments have land markets that are friendly enough to produce the required levels of planning gain needed to efficiently green economic development and make it financially viable to produce environmentally friendly patterns of settlement. These are sustainable because they guard the communities, undergoing development (the peripheral housing estate, former mining village and neighbourhoods) against everything that is seen to threaten them. This includes the coalescence of settlements, loss of identity, and break up of communities resulting from subsequent pressure for infill development and the urban sprawl, which this produces.

The reason why such questions need to be raised is simple. It is because in its current form, it is not possible to say whether the plan-led development is environmentally friendly or not. By effectively reducing the environmental values of the model to an aesthetic, it is simply not possible to say whether the design is friendly in terms of its ecological footprint, bio-diversity, or natural capital. Nor is it possible do say so in terms of the environmental loading, levels of energy consumption, bio-mass, waste, and emissions it produces. The fact is we simply do not know if the development is an environmental good or not!

Unless models of this type recognise such values, it will not be possible to say whether they are ecologically sound, only if their designs have land markets and levels of planning gain, which are friendly because they are efficient in 'greening' economic development. The danger is that in the absence of any environmental values, plan-led developments of this kind may become little more than an exercise in land marketing needed to produce the required levels of planning gain for an efficient greening of economic development. This may very well be financially viable, but for all that is still unable to substantiate the claims made about the environmentally friendly nature of the settlement pattern it produces insomuch that it guards against everything considered as a threat to the communities undergoing development.

Conclusions

It is evident the proposal to develop sustainable communities in Edinburgh's South East Wedge is transforming the new settlement phenomena in to a search for plan-led, environmentally friendly, and sustainable patterns of settlement. While clearly plan-led, there are a number of outstanding questions about the degree to which it is possible to define the nature of the development as environmentally friendly.

Set against the critique of such development models and the design solutions proposed, the paper has suggested that the environmental nature of the settlement pattern might be seen to add up to little more than an aesthetic. The chapter has sought to counter this representation of what is environmentally friendly by drawing attention to the environmental values of such models and the need for design solutions to concern themselves with the ecological footprint of the site, its bio-diversity, natural capital, and environmental loading. Furthermore, it has suggested that if environmental values concerning energy consumption, biomass, waste, and emissions of ecologically sound designs are considered key considerations in modelling the development of environmentally friendly settlement patterns, there is a clear need for them to be integrated into the models and the design solutions that are proposed.

Acknowledgement

The illustrations are reproduced with the kind permission of Edinburgh City Council.

References

Beatley, T., 1995. Planning and sustainability: the elements of a new (improved?) paradigm, *Journal of Planning Literature*, **9**(4).

Breheny, M., 1992a. The Compact City, *Built Environment*, **18**(4).

Breheny, M., 1992b. *Sustainable Development and Urban Forms*, Pion, London.

Brehney, M., 1995. Counter-urbanisation and sustainable urban forms. In: Brotchie, J (Ed.), *Cities in Competition*, Longman, Melbourne.

Breheny, M. and Rookwood R., 1993. Planning the sustainable city-region. In: Blowers, A (Ed.), *Planning for a Sustainable Environment*, Earthscan, London.

Breheny, M., Gent, T. and Lock, D., 1993. *Alternative Development Patterns: New Settlements*, HMSO, London.

Brown, F., 1998. Modelling urban growth, *Town and Country Planning*, November, 334-337.

Campbell, S., 1996. Green cities, growing cities, just cities?, *Journal of the American Planning Association*, **62**(4).

Cosgriff, B. and Steinemann, A., 1998. Industrial ecology for sustainable communities, *Journal of Environmental Planning and Management*, **41**(6).

Chesterton, 1996. *Edinburgh's South-East Wedge*. In: Final IDF Document, Chesterton Consulting, London.

Davoudi, S., 1997. Economic development and environmental gloss: a new structure plan for Lancashire. In: Brandon, P, Lombardi, P and Bentivenga V, (Eds.), *Evaluation of the Built Environment for Sustainability*, Chapman and Hall, London.

Deakin, M., 1996. Discounting, obsolescence, depreciation and their effects on the environment of cities, *Journal of Financial Management of Property and Construction*, **1**(2).

Deakin M., 1997. An economic evaluation and appraisal of the effects land use, building obsolescence and depreciation have on the environment of cities. In: Brandon, P, Lombardi, P and Bentivenga V, (Eds.), *Evaluation of the Built Environment for Sustainability*, Chapman and Hall, London.

Deakin, M., 1999a. Valuation, appraisal, discounting, obsolescence and depreciation: towards a life cycle analysis and impact assessment of their effects on the environment of cities, *International Journal of Life Cycle Assessment*, **4**(2).

Deakin, M., 1999b. The development of local authority property management: the search for the all-pervasive market, *Real Estate Valuation and Investment*, **3**(1).

Deakin, M., 2000. Developing sustainable communities in Edinburgh's South East Wedge', *Journal of Property Management*, **4**(2).

Deakin, M., 2002. Modelling the development of sustainable communities in Edinburgh's South East Wedge, *Planning Practice and Research*, **17**(3).

DoE., 1998. *Environmental Assessment* [Circular 15/88] HMSO, London.

DoE., 1991. *Policy Appraisal and the Environment*, HMSO, London.

DoE., 1993a. The Effectiveness of Green Belts, HMSO, London.

DoE., 1993b. *Reducing Transport Emissions through Planning*, HMSO, London.

DoE., 1993c. *Environmental Appraisal of Development Plans*, HMSO, London.

DoE., 1993d. *Making Markets Work for the Environment*, HMSO, London.

Glasson, J., Therival, R. and Chadwick, A., 1994. *Environmental Impact Assessment*, University College, London.

Gibbs, D., Longhurst, J. and Braithwaite, C., 1996. Moving towards sustainable development: integrating economic development and the environment in local authorities, *Journal of Environmental Planning and Management*, **39**(3).

Hall, P. and Ward, C., 1998. *Sociable Cities*, John Wiley, Chichester.

HM Government, 1990. *This Common Inheritance* HMSO, London.

HM Government, 1991. *This Common Inheritance* HMSO, London.

HM Government, 1994a. *This Common Inheritance* HMSO, London.

HM Government, 1994b. *Sustainable Development: The UK Strategy* HMSO, London.

Local Government Management Board, 1994. *Greening Economic Development*, LGMB, Luton.

Lothian Regional Council, 1994. *Structure Plan Review*, LRC, Edinburgh.

Ratcliffe, J. and Stubbs, M., 1996. *Urban Planning and Real Estate Development*, University College, London, London.

Selman, P., 1996. *Local Sustainability*, St. Martins Press, New York.

Ward, S., 1992. *Garden Cities, Past, Present and Future*, Spon, London.

Chapter 10

The Redevelopment of the Railway Lands of London's King's Cross: Actors, Agendas, and Processes

Emmanuel Mutale

Introduction

For more than 30 years, London's King's Cross railway lands have been the focus of various redevelopment proposals. Recent efforts to redevelop these lands date back to the 1970s. This was followed by another decade of proposals linked to the construction of the Channel Tunnel Rail Link (CTRL) terminus initially at King's Cross Station, then St Pancras. Current proposals are for a CTRL terminus, high-speed Kent commuter services at St Pancras, a new Thameslink station under St Pancras and new Thameslink connections to the Midland mainline, and East Coast mainline services. In addition, approximately 53 acres of land will also be available for redevelopment for uses other than rail infrastructure. In its entirety, King's Cross railway lands present one of the largest city centre development sites in Europe. The main thrust of this chapter is to identify a number of existing poles of interest, their respective agendas, and how these work to secure their own interests.

The number and kind of actors involved in the redevelopment process, including their interests, are strongly related to the specific circumstances under which this process takes place. For this reason the starting point is to set out the contextual policy background to current redevelopment proposals and then proceed to identify a methodological framework of analysis. The discussion then moves on to sketch the spatial context before identifying and analysing the roles/relationships and agendas of various actors and how they engage with the redevelopment process. Finally, an attempt is made to predict the effect of current and emerging central and local government policies on this redevelopment process.

British national planning framework

Development plans

In order to fully appreciate the redevelopment process at King's Cross, it is necessary to have an understanding of the planning system within which this is taking place. The nature of the British planning system has always been flexible and will almost always be so because of its liberal political system. The Town and Country Planning Act of 1990 (as amended) provides the key framework to guide the evolution of a rational land use pattern meant to serve public interests in Britain.

In London and other metropolitan areas, local authorities produce Unitary Development Plans (UDPs), which outline both strategic and detailed policy guidance for land development and also provide a basis for decisions on planning applications. A UDP consists of a Written Statement of general strategic policies and detailed local development control policies and proposals. In addition to the Written Statement, it also incorporates a Proposals Map, which shows the sites to which development proposals and policies relate.

Public participation

While there are issues about the nature of public involvement in the planning process, public participation has been a feature of the British planning system since the early 1970s following the Skeffington Report of 1969. This report recommended that development plans should be based on democratically agreed proposals and thus advocated the involvement of all stakeholders - including local people - affected by the development plan proposals. Present guidance on the preparation of development plans requires that local authorities incorporate in their plan preparation, two six-week periods during which the public can examine and if necessary object to any proposals. These two periods are known as the first and second deposit stages. Issues remaining unresolved between the public, the local authority and any other interested party after the second stage are brought before the planning inquiry, at which an independent planning inspector sits to hear from, and arbitrate between, the various interests. It is also common for local authorities to consult on a pre-deposit draft of the development plan.

Major infrastructure projects

While local authorities have planning and development control powers within their own areas of jurisdiction, major infrastructure projects such as motorways, railways, airports etc., whose effects are more widespread - spanning more than one local authority - are subject to different processes. Decisions in these cases are made by Parliament through a number of different procedures.

Major infrastructure projects often fall under a variety of statutory regimes, principally the Town and Country Planning Act 1990, the Transport and Works Act 1992, the Highways Act 1980, the Harbours Act 1964, and the Electricity Act

106 *Methodologies, Models and Instruments*

1989. Two procedures are normally employed in informing Parliament of major infrastructure project proposals and obtaining Parliamentary approval for them.

Private Bill. Where the nature of the proposal is restricted to a particular group of people such as a local authority or private company. That particular group drafts a Private Bill and nominates a Member of Parliament (MP) to introduce the bill on their behalf. Persons objecting to proposals in a Private Bill can, under special procedures, petition Parliament. Petitions are heard by a panel of MPs who decide whether to accept or reject the petitions;

Hybrid Bill. Sometimes development proposals will affect private organisations or individuals, local and wider public interests. For example, the CTRL was conceived as a private sector led project but with government financial support whose potential social, economic and environmental impacts were going to be manifest all along the proposed route and stations. The Bill is debated by the House of Commons and the House of Lords and individuals and organisations are also allowed an opportunity to set forth their case to select committees constituted from each House.

Policy Planning Guidance

The British government publishes thematic Policy Planning Guidance (PPG) notes to assist with the planning process. Current PPG notes run from 1 to 25 with PPG1 dedicated to General Policy and Principles, PPG3 to housing, PPG12 to Development Plans, etc.

In addition, Regional Planning Guidance (RPG) notes are also published for each of the eight English regions. Relevant to this Chapter is the Regional Planning Guidance for the South East (RPG9) published in March 2001. While RPG9 talks about focusing new development around transport nodes, RPG3 explicitly refers to King's Cross as a major development opportunity.

Proposed changes to the British planning system

The basic structure of the present planning system, the 1947 Act as modified in 1991, is now thought to be too inflexible, bureaucratic, and unsuited to meaningful public participation. Consultation has ended (18 March 2002) on a Green Paper published by the Department of Transport, Local Government and the Regions (DTLR, 2001) intended to deliver fundamental reforms to the British Planning process. It is proposed to simplify the process by replacing the need for a whole hierarchy of local plans, with Action Plans based on new Local Development Frameworks, linked to local Community Strategy, all of which will be prepared in partnership with the local community. It is also intended to make the new system more efficient and predictable for business applications.

There are also proposals for changes to the Parliamentary procedures for making decisions on major infrastructure projects because the current system is said to take too long, and be expensive and adversarial. Of course, leaving decisions on major infrastructure to Parliament has the potential to politicise issues and risks decisions being made on political expediency rather than technical arguments. The Green Paper recognises this and there is an attempt to make procedures more explicit. It can also be argued that political decisions can also be technically well informed and benefit from quick decisions based on the reasoning that Parliament has a broad constituency and legitimacy.

Regional governance

The creation of the new Greater London Authority (GLA) in June 2000 added a layer of regional governance on London. The GLA Act of 1999 requires the Mayor to produce the following strategies: spatial development, transport, regeneration, municipal waste, air quality, ambient noise, bio-diversity, and culture. Of interest to our discussion is the Spatial Development Strategy (SDS), which set within the national planning policy framework, provides among other things, a strategic framework for the local UDPs. As such, it recommends a 50% quota of affordable housing development and, while replacing RPG3, it retains the latter's view of high density development around public transport nodes.

Analytical framework

The planning triangle (Figure 10.1) as developed by Bertolini and Spit (1998) is used. It facilitates the study of an area by looking at the problem from three related perspectives (context, process, and object). While remaining focused, the framework is also broad enough to draw in the most relevant issues in the study of redevelopment proposals. The 'object' perspective of the framework relates to King's Cross, not only as a transport node, but also as a place in its own right. The 'context' perspective sets the study within the national, regional, and local policy arena and explores how this might impact on the redevelopment proposals. The 'process' perspective is elaborated and applied to study the approaches of various actors, in their attempts to drive their own agendas forward.

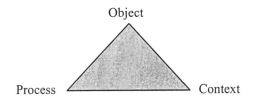

Figure 10.1 The Planning Triangle
Source: Bertolini and Spit, 1998

108 *Methodologies, Models and Instruments*

Spatial context

The King's Cross railway lands (Figure 10.2) - also known as King's Cross Central - is a great swathe of land up to 135 acres in extent, about 35-53 acres of which are available for redevelopment other than rail infrastructure. The difference between the total extent and what is available for redevelopment reflects the huge land take required for the railway infrastructure.

Situated in central London and on a leading transport node, King's Cross Central is described as Europe's largest regeneration project. The southern extent of the site can be roughly defined as Euston Road, and King's Cross and St Pancras Stations - two important railway stations built at the height of the railway revolution in the mid 1800s to provide a passenger and freight link between London, the Northern, Midlands, and Scotland.

Apart from being important mainline rail termini and interchange with other transport nodes, the place also served as a strong distribution point for the rest of London. However, subsequent heavy railway disinvestment and structural economic changes have combined with indecision over the CTRL since 1986 to produce the blight that is evident in the area today. The rest of the boundaries are the Midland Road and the Midland Main line to the west, the North London railway line to the north and York Way to the east. The Regents Canal running approximately east to west bisects the Railway lands.

Activities to the north of the canal include storage and distribution, temporary leisure activities (such as a golf driving range and go-kart track), concrete batching plants, vehicle depots, and repair operations. Adjoining the canal to the south-west is the Camley Street Nature Park. The King's Cross railway lands lie almost entirely within the London Borough of Camden (LBC) although a small area east of York Way, known as the Islington triangle, lies within the London Borough of Islington (LBI).

Two-thirds of the railway lands lie within two conservation areas. There are also a number of listed buildings graded according to the priority of protection - with grade 1 being the highest. St Pancras Station/St Pancras Chambers, King's Cross Station are listed as grade 1, the Great Northern Hotel, German Gymnasium, 4 gas holders, Lock-Keeper's cottage, and granary are grade 2 listed. The Camley Street Nature Park is part of the Regent's Canal conservation area. Outside the railway lands area are a number of additional buildings and structures of supplementary architectural and historical interest that are part of the King's Cross Conservation area. The challenge this presents is for a redevelopment scheme that does not conflict with the area's rich Victorian heritage in terms of scale and design.

The Redevelopment of the Railway Lands of King's Cross 109

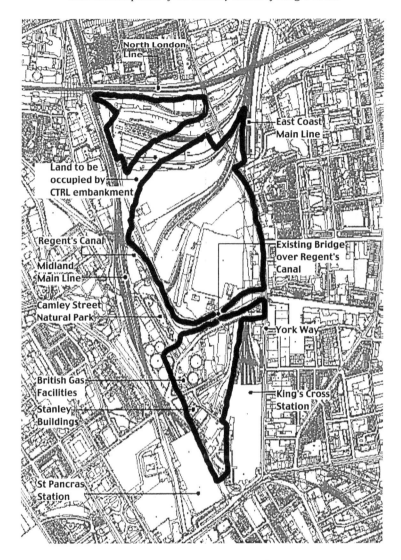

Figure 10.2 King's Cross railway lands site boundary
Source: Argent St George, December 2001

Actors, agendas and processes

This section examines a number of the key actors, their interests, and relationships. From a whole array of actors, a deliberate decision has been taken to focus on those deemed to be the most influential and directly relevant to the redevelopment of King's Cross Central. These are LBC, in whose jurisdiction the greater part of the lands falls, LCR, and the King's Cross Railway Lands Group (KXRLG).

London and Continental Railways (LCR) Limited

LCR is a consortium made up of Eurostar (UK) Limited, Union Railways Limited, and London and Continental Stations and Property Limited. In 1996 LCR won the competitive bid to build and operate the CTRL - UK's first major new railway for over a hundred years - and to own and operate Eurostar (UK) Limited - the UK arm of the Eurostar train service from London to Paris and Brussels. The new international rail link has to be privately financed. In addition to carrying international Eurostar trains, the CTRL would also carry Kent commuter trains - a proposition seen by others as a backdoor subsidy to LCR for the construction of the track and stations.

With the estimated cost in the region of at least £5 billion, the commercial value of the project is a significant factor in securing private finance. As envisaged by the government's structuring of the bidding process, LCR's agenda therefore is to maximise the commercial value of, and return on, their landholdings, and the operational success of CTRL. However, in February 1998, LCR's funding initiative collapsed through a failure to raise private finance. In June 1998 The Secretary of State for the Environment, in a complex rescue package (involving government backed bonds and a subsidy (KXRLG, July 1998) announced that the £5.4 billion rail link would be built in two sections (Figure 10.3). The first section would stretch from Folkestone to Fawkham Junction in North Kent and then onto existing tracks to London's Waterloo station. The second and more expensive section would terminate at St Pancras with new international stations at Ebbsfleet and Stratford.

On 31 March 2000, LCR announced the appointment of two development partners from a final short list of three competing companies:

- Argent Group PLC - a leading commercial developer in the UK whose portfolio includes Brindleyplace near the centre of Birmingham, and the Thames Valley Park in Reading;
- St George PLC - another UK leader in residential development with a focus on inner city regeneration schemes.

The Redevelopment of the Railway Lands of King's Cross 111

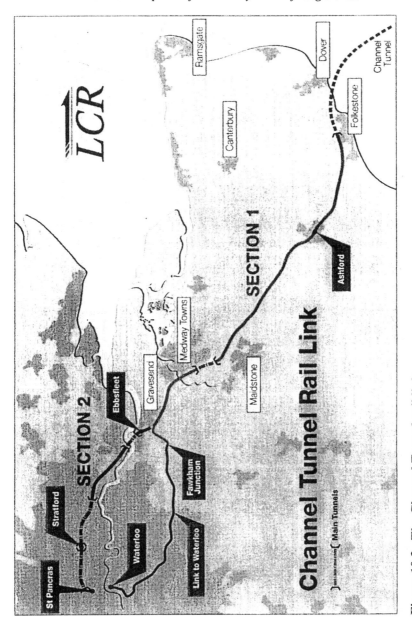

Figure 10.3 The Channel Tunnel rail link
Source: KXRLG Annual Report, 98/99

112 *Methodologies, Models and Instruments*

It does appear that from the moment LCR won the bid they knew that they would have problems. In an effort to give the redevelopment proposal a new start and distance it from the stop-start schemes of the 1980s, and the tense and fraught exchanges of the past, LCR re-christened the King's Cross railway lands as King's Cross Central. This is not to suggest that from now on all was going to be well. On 11 November 2000, the Daily Telegraph reported that Railtrack - a key funder of CTRL section 2 - had asked government for more money, arguing that the project was going to cost them a lot more than £2.5 billion. This temporarily put the certainty of CTRL in doubt yet again. As if this were not enough, a National Audit Report published in March 2001 was scathing of the rail link, dismissing it as not being good value for money (Network, July 2001). In April 2001, LCR, the government, and Railtrack signed an agreement confirming the financial arrangements for section 2 of CTRL and, thus, putting to rest - for the moment - funding uncertainties that had plagued this project.

Following the appointment of the two development partners, LCR have been determined to be seen to be consulting. Local people on the other hand, have been concerned that this form of consultation should not be a mere window dressing exercise in which the community was only asked to participate in so-called 'Mickey Mouse' issues but not in the strategic ones.

By July 2001, it was certain that things were happening. Major engineering work had begain; shops affected by the works were boarded up after the tenants had been asked to leave; residential tenants in housing blocks affected by the works were in the process of being moved out; and work to dismantle gas holders had also began. In addition, the developer, LCR and other landowners published the first public consultation document titled, *Principles for a Human City* (Argent St George, July 2001) outlining ten principles formulated to:

> fulfil the commercial imperative to optimise the economic value of the land and the King's Cross redevelopment. This, in turn, will provide the means to optimise community benefits and our contribution to meeting local needs.

This first consultation document was also intended as part of the developer's contribution to Chapter 13 of Camden's UDP review process, which outlines policies for the railway lands. Building on the first consultation and other studies, the second consultation report, *Parameters for Regeneration* (Argent St George, December 2001) listed 13 parameters intended to provide a reference document sketching out with minimum technical detail some of the master planning guiding elements. Some of these parameters relate to planning policy, CTRL works, land use and density, physical, and social integration, heritage, and environment. A third consultation document, *A Framework for Regeneration* (Argent St George, September 2002) presented the developer's range of development options, ideas on the relationship between space and movement within the project area, and how this connected with adjoining areas. The hope is that people will be better informed to debate and appraise the developer's master planning proposals when these begin to emerge and are submitted for planning permission in 2003.

The Redevelopment of the Railway Lands of King's Cross   113

LCR hopes that the continuous search for consensus through an iterative consultation process will give the planning application an easy ride and thus avoid the lengthy public inquiries. The finalised master plan has to link into Camden's UDP, build upon existing studies such as the Site Implementation Study (SIS - discussed below), and take account of the Greater London Authority's Spatial Development Strategy.

Up to now, the developer has shown a willingness to consult and has also engaged a consultant to advise on how to gain 'Good Corporation' status, accorded by the Institute of Business Ethics, for demonstrating socially responsible behaviour. The indicative timetable is that the construction of section 2 of the CTRL, having begun in 2001, will end in 2006 with high-speed services to and from St Pancras commencing early 2007. The complete redevelopment of the railway lands for uses other than rail infrastructure may take up to 15 years to complete.

London Borough of Camden - LBC

LBC is one of the two local planning authorities in whose jurisdiction the railway lands fall (the other is LBI) and is concerned to see through its adopted and evolving local and strategic planning policy. Although LBC are the local planning authority, they cannot obstruct the strategic idea of CTRL because this had its approval through an act of Parliament in 1996. What LBC can do is only to decide on the balance of land uses on the remainder of the railway lands after the CTRL is built, and other issues related to work practices and environmental pollution. While other London boroughs secured agreement on their UDPs early on, Camden's UDP was only adopted in March 2000 - five years later than the forecast adoption date of 1995/6. This delay was partly due to indecision on CTRL and several objections, principally seeking a greater community benefit through the provision of more affordable housing on the railway lands. Camden's UDP sets out - among other things - strategic policies for the railway lands. Concerned about the scale and possible impacts of the redevelopment of the Railway lands, LBC commissioned a detailed SIS to add to the November 1994 adopted Community Planning Brief for the site, the UDP, and Strategic Planning Guidance as material planning considerations for the redevelopment of these lands. The SIS was published in November 1997 with the principal requirement of:

> clarifying, analysing and assessing the development constraints and potential of the King's Cross Railway lands and provide advice on the practical steps that should be taken to secure their earliest possible comprehensive regeneration (KXRLG Annual Report 96/97: p12).

The railway lands are seen by Camden - whose historic position is that of a rate-capped inner London authority - as a sole opportunity to gain national and international prestige and investment. Camden's UDP reflects this by designating the King's Cross railway lands as an Opportunity Area and devotes the whole of Chapter 13 of its UDP to elaborate site-specific policies designed to give guidance

114 *Methodologies, Models and Instruments*

for their redevelopment. The core strategic statement for the area says that LBC aims to:

> ...seek a comprehensive approach to the redevelopment of the King's Cross Opportunity Area, which maximises the large-scale potential contribution which the site can make to London's commercial prosperity and its attractiveness to tourists, and which provides benefits to neighbouring communities in terms of housing and supporting services, and measures to enhance local access to employment. It must integrate well with its surroundings, both socially and physically, and address the capacity restraints imposed by the existing public transport systems and road network. Such development will be based on principles of sustainability, ensuring mixed use development which respects the industrial heritage of the site, gives priority to good design and secures efficient transport interchange facilities (Camden UDP, 2000: 267).

London Borough of Camden's UDP base line was the 1991 Census date. As it became obvious that the redevelopment of the railway lands was going ahead, it was necessary to quickly review the plan to ensure that not only would it address matters identified by the UDP Inspector for early review. Furthermore, it would also provide the developers with an up-to-date reference framework based on a current understanding of local issues and one which took account of regional institutional and policy changes brought about by the formation of the GLA. To get the most important changes through quickly, the review process was split into three parts: Chapter 13, UDP policies for affordable housing; and finally the main body. Following a period of consultation, Camden issued final proposals for a revised Chapter 13, *King's Cross Opportunity Area* in November 2001. The following are the main changes in the revised Chapter 13:

- the proportion of affordable housing was raised from 25-50% to a minimum of 50%. In terms of units, from 930-1000 units to a minimum of 1000 units;
- there was also a strong emphasis on car-free housing units; and
- more on community regeneration and 'green' issues.

The developer's response to the affordable homes quota has been to warn that this might drive them away. The Chief Executive of Argent was quoted as saying:

> This kind of bold statement could drive developers out. It could make the whole thing unviable and if we would not do it and then nobody would do it (Hampstead and Highgate Express, 8 March 2002).

While such a statement might cause concern with LBC, the community group KXRLG does not seem to want be held to such ransom.

King's Cross railway lands Group (KXRLG)

The KXRLG is a voluntary umbrella organisation of more than 300 individuals, groups, and businesses in LBC and LBI. The organisation is concerned with the redevelopment of the railway lands, and how to ensure the local community benefits from the redevelopment. The group has had an aggressive but positive interest in local development issues since 1987, and has a reasonable level of understanding and analysis of the issues: they have attacked planning policies and proposed alternatives. The main concern of the KXRLG is to secure a 'New Urban Quarter' development that is sensitive, appropriate, and of lasting benefit to those who live and work in the area (KXRLG Annual Report 95/96). KXRLG interpretation of this is:

> an Urban Village (mixed uses, mixed tenures), containing thousands of new homes, jobs, community and leisure facilities of all kinds... (KXRLG Annual Report 97/98:15).

This KXRLG argues, accords with Strategic Guidance, government policy for brownfield sites, Camden's adopted Planning Brief and UDP (KXRLG, February 1998). Edwards (1999: p3) articulates the benefits of mixed-use thus:

> Workers in the daytime and residents in the evenings and weekends help to support pubs, shops, buses, nurseries, clinics etc. They keep the streets peopled and can share the same (few) car parks. Students (and educational users generally) use space and bedrooms at times of year, which are complementary with the tourist seasons. Many cultural bodies can make use of performance and exhibition spaces in interlocking rhythms.

Concerned about the continued blight resulting from the lack of redevelopment, but also worried about the adverse effects of an international terminus at St Pancras, the KXRLG has shifted from one view to another. However, the view from within the group is that is not a shift but that the group has always had both a local and strategic perspective. The local view relates to the redevelopment of the railway lands with no reference to the international terminus. This view argues that redevelopment of the railway lands is not dependent upon the CTRL international terminus at St Pancras (KXRLG Annual Report, 97/98). The presence of 135 acres of brownfield land at a transport node in inner London is an incentive enough for any developer. The strategy focuses on an international terminus at Stratford with a possible shuttle service between Stratford and St Pancras. Up until April 2000 KXRLG was liasing with the City of London Corporation, Thames Gateway Partnership and the London Borough of Newham on a campaign for a CTRL terminal/interchange station at Stratford. This would link CTRL to CrossRail, a Stratford to Paddington proposal passing through Liverpool Street, Farringdon, Tottenham Court Road, and Bond Street. When in 1996, LCR were appointed to develop and operate the CTRL, the group saw this as an important development. This was especially so since prior to winning the bid to build and operate the

116 *Methodologies, Models and Instruments*

CTRL, LCR were not in favour of an international terminus at St Pancras. This position was seen as less damaging for the local community than Union Rail's (a British Rail subsidiary) earlier proposals to bring CTRL into and under King's Cross. Shortly after LCR's appointment, KXRLG met with the former hopeful of developing a constructive relationship with regard to the CTRL and the Railway lands. KXRLG's concerns about the international terminus at St Pancras related to:

- the temporary and permanent displacement of households and businesses with little or no compensation;
- severe disruption and environmental impacts during the at least 5-year construction period; and
- the risk of altering the conservation character of the area due to the possible demolition of listed buildings, incompatible designs and the impact of a radically changed economic base upon the prevailing local and cultural character of the area.

Although the war is certainly not yet won, the group has won a few battles along the way. For example, it has managed to secure agreement for undertakings and assurances to be included in the Code of Construction of the CTRL Act to restrict construction work to certain hours and thus minimise disturbances from construction traffic (KXRLG Annual Report, 96/97). Its strong stand on social and environment issues has secured the consideration of these criteria in an industry dominated by 'business for profit' accounting principles. LCR's stated position is that the landowner sets the framework for redevelopment and then consults (LCR, 1999). The view of the KXRLG is that the community works with the master planners through 'planning for real' and similar approaches - planning activities in which the community is presented with a *Tabula Rasa* (empty piece of land) and asked to indicate what they want built where.

In March 2000, KXRLG cautiously welcomed the appointment of Argent St George by LCR as development partners for the railway lands with the hope that these lands were at last going to be redeveloped. The KXRLG however, remained concerned about the balance between social and commercial benefits of the resulting development, especially since the private developers had been asked to contribute £1 billion to the total cost of the second phase of the CTRL into St Pancras (KXRLG Annual Report, 99/00). It was now becoming certain that the CTRL would, after all, be arriving in St Pancras. This led the group to tacitly acknowledge this development by pledging that whatever happens to the Crossrail/CTRL debate, it would continue with its community advocacy work by monitoring Argent St George plans to secure benefits for the local people (KXRLG Annual Report, 99/00).

Following a succession of unfortunate events - the departure of the group's office administrator; the death of the group's treasurer; reduced funding from LBC; and the loss of its office space - all coming towards the end of the year 2000, the organisation's continued existence was severely tested. Indeed it even failed to form a new committee at its October 2000 Annual General Meeting, deciding instead to form a steering group to develop a Strategy for Survival. At a time when developments related to the railway lands were gaining momentum, the group was struggling to survive. Where once it could initiate its own planning proposals for the railway lands, the group was now only able to deal reactively with developments. Indeed attempts at a 'real planning' exercise foundered due to the lack of resources and support within the group.

By April 2001, the KXRLG was beginning to be more explicit about the inevitability of CTRL at St Pancras. It decided to focus its energies on securing community benefits through a constructive engagement with the developer and LBC - having an input in the master planning consultation process and responding to LBC's review of its UDP. In its contribution to the review of Chapter 13 of LBC's UDP, the group made a number of proposals. These included:

- a safe, mixed-use development that improves on and maximises the existing public transport network;
- that housing built on the railway lands should be split equally between affordable and other housing;
- that as well as development befitting London's claim to be a world city, the area's rich heritage should be respected; and
- a proposal that companies moving into the redeveloped railway lands be required to draw a quarter of their labour force locally, and also provide training.

When the final draft of Chapter 13 was circulated for consultation by LBC in November 2001, KXRLG while expressing misgivings about the fast speed with which the review process was proceeding, gave it a cautious welcome noting that most of the group's suggestions had been taken on board. After a turbulent 2001, the group seemed to be settling down after finding new office space, engaging a part-time office administrator and securing some funding.

In its attempts to influence development proposals, the KXRLG has used a number of strategies, e.g. newsletters, the media, fielding of petitions, and representation at public enquiries. The strength of KXRLG's attempts to influence the development proposals at King's Cross derive from expert knowledge of the local area, local planning procedures, policies brought in by its strong but narrow professional base, and community leaders. Although committed to a community-led development of the railway lands, the one weakness the group still has to overcome is the perception of it being narrowly representative. KXRLG has not maintained a strong grassroots base and as people have moved on or retired the group is increasingly finding it hard to sustain its influence. This was exacerbated by the reduction in its grant from LBC, and the loss of cheap office space in the latter part of 2000. The group openly admits that it has found it difficult to involve all sectors of the community it represents, especially the disadvantaged groups (KXRLG Annual Reports, 96/97; 97/98; 98/99).

118 *Methodologies, Models and Instruments*

What next?

Although the Mayor's housing report published in November 2000 recommends a target of 50% affordable housing, RPG prioritises business development. With rail companies under pressure to maximise their profits, keen to create a rival new quarter for London, and coy about the benefits of a mixed-use redevelopment, retail and office space might dominate the redevelopment of the railway lands at King's Cross.

The present rates structure gives no incentive to local authorities to support non-residential development proposals but, because of the reduced planning powers and fears of costly litigation, even a community-conscious authority like LBC could be under pressure to accommodate private developers. The existing rates structure means that the burden of managing these areas will fall on the local authority without an assured corresponding financial gain. There is need for adequate mechanisms for capturing increased land values brought about by planning permission.

It can already be seen that the certainty of CTRL happening is displacing some businesses affected by these proposals. As the area regenerates and rents increase, those businesses unable to compete might contract, close, or relocate leading to a loss or displacement of jobs with little or no gain for local communities. King's Cross Central runs the risk of attracting the same criticisms as Docklands - a property redevelopment criticised for its limited benefits to the local community.

The redevelopment of the Stratford marshalling yards, which the CTRL might stimulate, might create more employment opportunities in East London, thus contributing to a balance of opportunities between the east and west of London. Regional metro-type schemes (Crossrail and Thameslink) would generate benefits for Londoners, but would also facilitate the further growth of long-distance commuting, which is part of the labour-market problem confronting low-skill London residents who often seem to be overlooked in favour of suburban recruits. For this reason, employment opportunities created at Stratford or St Pancras might not actually help the job situation for Londoners.

Conclusions

Urban redevelopment or regeneration is as much about people as place, and processes as well as product. As more actors get involved not only is it increasingly likely that interests might diverge, but also that the planning and implementation process is lengthened. The time it takes to bring about a redevelopment of this scale is therefore related to the level of conflict/understanding, which develops between these interests. This chapter identified three main poles of interest groups in King's Cross - LCR, LBC, and KXRLG. Except for LCR, all other interests are largely local. LCR's interests, on the other hand, go beyond the local to include London-wide, national, and international concerns. KXRLG has built a high profile and has had significant influence over local (and CTRL) planning policy. Although it is argued in the regeneration discourse that successful structures seem to have local roots, it is important that this is balanced with a wider strategic role. A high profile locality such as King's Cross is expected to play such a role in the regional, national, or international context, yet do so without compromising the needs of the local community.

The discussion reveals the confrontations, compromises, deals, and tactical alliances that have characterised the redevelopment proposals at King's Cross. It may be difficult in this context to ensure that each and every interest is addressed. Nonetheless, it is essential that redevelopment meets the needs and aspirations of both the landowners, developers and those of the majority of local residents and working population. Presently, there is no clearly established system to link the various cascading levels of interests and where they conflict, a mechanism for mediation. The discussions have also sought to show that these strong cleavages are at the same time malleable - can be influenced, modified etc. For example, LCR is now able to take account of social aspects in its proposal and is keen to be seen to consult with the community - however inadequate this might be seen to be. On the other hand, although KXRLG had resisted an international terminus at St Pancras, there is evidence of a pragmatic shift on this stance shown by their acknowledgement of the possibility of this happening.

This discussion represents an attempt to contribute to the existing discourse on urban politics in King's Cross. If, or when the railway lands are redeveloped, one should be able to look back and analyse the negotiated outcome of this major scheme and how this relates to the agendas, resources, influences, and interplay of various interest groups.

Acknowledgements

I would like to thank my colleagues Michael Edwards, Michael Parkes, and others in the Bartlett School of Planning at University College London for their detailed comments on the draft of this paper.

References

Argent St George, July 2001. *Principles for a Human City.*
Argent St George, December 2001. *Parameters for Regeneration.*
Argent St George, September 2002. *A Framework for Regeneration.*
Bertolini, L. and Spit, T., 1998. *Cities on Rails: The Redevelopment of Railway Station Areas,* London.
CUDP, 2000. Camden Unitary Development Plan.
DTLR, 2001. *Planning Green Paper.*
Edwards, M. 1999. *A Real Plan for King's Cross.* UCL, Bartlett School of Planning. http://www.bartlett.ucl.ac.uk/courses/kx/realKX.htm
Hampstead and Highgate Express, 8 March 2002.
KXRLG *Annual Report, 95/96.*

KXRLG *Annual Report, 96/97.*
KXRLG *Annual Report, 97/98.*
KXRLG *Annual Report, 98/99.*
KXRLG *Annual Report, 99/00.*
KXRLG, February 1998. *Our position on the Channel Tunnel Rail Link.*
KXRLG *Newsletter*, July 1998.
KXRLG *Newsletter*, Network, July 2001.
LCR, 1999. *Land Owner's Brief - King's Cross Central*, Revision 1.

Chapter 11

BEQUEST: Sustainable Urban Development, the Framework, and Directory of Assessment Methods

Mark Deakin and Steve Curwell

Introduction

This chapter documents the interim findings of the BEQUEST (Building Environmental Quality Evaluation for Sustainability) network and the project's investigation of sustainable urban development. The network has its origins in an international conference, held in Florence in 1995, *The Environmental Impact of Buildings and Cities* (Brandon, *et al.*, 1997). More recently, the network has been funded from the Research Directorate of the EU 4th Framework Programme. The project sets out to develop a common language and approach to Sustainable Urban Development (SUD) and aims to produce a framework, directory of assessment methods, and set of procurement protocols for such purposes.

The framework, assessment methods, and procurement protocols are currently in the process of being linked together as a tool-kit. It is anticipated this instrument will used by those advising on the sustainability of urban development and taking decisions about the city of tomorrow and its cultural heritage. Collectively, this is aimed at building environmental capacity, qualifying and evaluating the sustainability of urban development. Reporting on this recent manifestation of BEQUEST, the chapter:

- outlines the areas of the Environment and Climate Programme (Economic and Social Aspects of Human Settlement) addressed by the BEQUEST project;
- examines the framework the project has developed as a basis for a common understanding of SUD; and
- provides a post-Brundtland directory of the assessment methods currently made use of to build environmental capacity.

The environment and climate programme

Although BEQUEST is a 4th Framework project, it addresses Action 4: the City of Tomorrow and Cultural Heritage of the EU Environment and Climate Programme in the 5th Framework. The aims and objectives of the BEQUEST project relate to Section 4.1 of the City of Tomorrow and Cultural Heritage. It is also relevant to Section 4.3 and the paragraphs particularly refer to sustainable development, resource conservation, and environmental protection. In terms of the EU's document, *Sustainable Urban Development: a Framework for Action* (CEU, 1998), the project also raises awareness of SUD. This is achieved through exploring ways of utilising communication and information technology, to exchange experiences in framing the relevant issues and assessing the effect resource conservation and environmental protection has upon the city of tomorrow and its cultural heritage.

The BEQUEST project and methodology

The 1992 EC programme of policy and action clearly identifies the need to study sustainable development as a priority, particularly in terms of reconciling the conflicting demands of urbanisation with those of resource conservation and environmental protection. The BEQUEST concerted action project aims to lay the foundations for a common understanding of sustainable urban development through a multi-disciplinary network of contributions from the scientific and professional communities.

 The research method adopted by the action programme provides a structured process of interaction between the wide range of interests involved in the process of urban development (i.e. the planning, provision, use and maintenance of the built environment as a form of human settlement). Mature deliberation, debate and evolution are key elements of the project and develop through an iterative learning cycle of workshops, reflection and concerted action. The project partners, known as the Intranet, act as the mentors and facilitators of this process. Extranet members participate in the project though the workshops and by means of follow-up comments on information papers. Using communication systems, including a web page, the workshops provide the project partners and extranet members with the information technology needed for the networked community to debate sustainable urban development and enter into a dialogue about both resource conservation and environmental protection.

 Together, the intranet and extranet represent the type of networked community required to build environmental capacity, qualify whether the city of tomorrow is able to carry its cultural heritage and evaluate if the forms of human settlement resulting from this process of urban development are sustainable. There are 14 partners in the BEQUEST EU project and over 130 extranet members in the networked community. To date, 6 international workshops have been held (Milton Keynes, Amsterdam, Turin, Helsinki, Florence, Vienna) and further details of this work, together with the associated information papers, can be found at the

Sustainable Urban Development 123

following web-site address: http://www.surveying.salford.ac.uk/bq/extra. The web-site also provides an outline of the project, the partners and extranet members.

This chapter concentrates upon two of the project objectives: the framework for a common understanding of sustainable urban development, and directory of assessment methods.

A framework for a common understanding

As any standard textbook on environmental issues points out, sustainable development is difficult to define. The first commonly accepted meaning of the term was that offered by the Brundtland Report, which defines it as:

> development that meets the needs of the present without compromising the ability of future generations to meet their own needs (WCED, 1987).

Subsequently the UN 'Earth Summit' held in Rio in 1992, developed a wider concept known as Agenda 21 and is represented in shorthand form as Figure 11.1 (Mitchell, *et al.*, 1995, as developed by Cooper, 1997). Here attention is drawn to concerns about the quality of the environment, the equity of resource consumption, as well as the participation of the public in decisions taken concerning the future urban development process, the city of tomorrow, and its cultural heritage. It is this four-fold representation (environment, equity, participation, and futurity) of sustainable development that the BEQUEST project has adopted.

Following the issue of 'human settlement', which appeared in the Brundtland Report, Agenda 21, and the UN Habitat Conference in 1996, the project has sought to draw upon these definitions as a means of moving the EU towards a framework for a common understanding of sustainable urban development. In Europe, human settlement is predominantly urban in form (with two-thirds of EU citizens living in towns or cities) and as a consequence, questions about sustainable development relate to matters concerning the future of the development of urban futures, cities of tomorrow, and their cultural heritage. They are questions about how to build the capacity needed, not only to conserve resources and protect the environment, but qualify and evaluate whether such actions are equitable and dealt with in an manner that fosters public participation in decisions taken over the future of urban development.

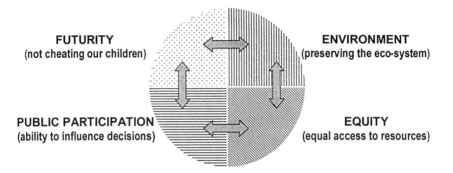

Figure 11.1 The underlying issues of sustainable development
Source: adapted from Cooper (1997)

Fore-grounding the urban question

The project has sought to identify the common issues underlying the growing interest in sustainable development and structure them to provide a framework for analysis (Nijkamp, 1991; Mitchell *et al.*, 1995; Mega, 1996; Miltin and Satterhwaite, 1996; and Pugh, 1996). This has been achieved by initially adopting the Mitchell, *et al.* (1995) definition of sustainable development, 'mapping out' the 'fuzzy buzzwords' (Palmer, *et al.*, 1997), and by then modifying it to include the underlying issues of urbanisation. This modification has required:

- fore-grounding the question of urban development (Nijkamp, 1991) and representing the process of urbanisation as a life cycle of inter-related activities;
- agreeing the issues of sustainable development (Mega, 1996; Miltin and Satterhwaite, 1996) underlying the urban process; and
- identifying the environmental, economic and social structure, spatial level, and time scales of sustainable urban development (Pugh, 1996).

The project has sub-divided the development process by a division of labour between the scientific and professional communities. With respect to urban development, the division of labour is that of urban development; planning, design, construction, and operation (use, demolition, and recycling). Representing the process of urbanisation as a life cycle of inter-related activities, the sustainable development issues that surface concern the environmental, economic, and social structure, spatial level, and time scales of SUD. The spatial level of analysis identifies the territorial impact of urban development. This illustrates that the impact can be at the city, district, neighbourhood, estate, building, and component and material level. The consideration of time-scales also shows that the impact can be short, medium, and long-term in nature.

Towards a directory of environmental assessment methods

While fore-grounding provides a framework for analysis, it does not address the question of how decision-makers can reverse the current trend of resource depletion, conserve resources, and protect the environment? To achieve this it is necessary to:

- assess whether the environmental capacity (ecological integrity, equity, participation and futurity) required for the city of tomorrow to carry its cultural heritage, currently exists; and
- qualify and evaluate whether the forms of human settlement that develop are sustainable. This raises the question of what assessment methods are currently available for such purposes? A further question is whether they can, on their own or in combination with others, be drawn upon to build the environmental capacity needed to both qualify and evaluate if the forms of human settlement which develop are sustainable?

In addressing this question, the networked community has agreed the sustainable development issues underlying the process of urbanisation. These have been defined in terms of their environmental, economic, social, and institutional components. Environmental issues take on the form of considerations about how the process of urbanisation consumes natural resources, whether it produces emissions that pollute the atmosphere and the effect, which development of this kind has upon the bio-diversity of habitats. Economic considerations relate to questions about the financing of the infrastructures, transport, and utilities required for the built environment to accommodate the urban development process and employment of resources associated with this. The social issues concern matters about access to such services, the safety and security of cities, human health and well-being cultural heritage provides. The institutional issues refer to the governance, justice, and ethics of settlement patterns subject to urban development.

The reason why sustainable development issues, their spatial levels, and time scales raise questions about environmental assessment is of particular significance. This is because many of the assessment methods currently in existence are pre-Brundtland and, in their present form, do not adequately address the questions of resource conservation, environmental capacity, or sustainable development. Many of the assessment methods currently in existence can be traced back to cost-benefit analysis and the critique of the discounting principle it is based upon (Pearce and Markauya, 1989; Pearce and Turner, 1990; Norgaard and Howarth, 1991; Rydin, 1992; Deakin, 1996; 1997; 1999). Their development can also be linked to the emergence of hedonic and non-market techniques of analysis as alternative forms of assessment.

Following the Brundtland Report, the science of environmental assessment has been placed under investigation by the green movement, and critical distinctions have been drawn between eco and anthropocentric techniques of

126 *Methodologies, Models and Instruments*

analysis (Pearce and Warford, 1993). The former incorporates the ecological systems making up the environment, which the anthropology of human settlement (in all its economic, social and institutional forms) is understood to depend. Since the Rio Earth Summit, attention has turned to the concept of 'ecological footprint' and its use as a means of assessing the capacity the environment has to carry the city of tomorrow (Rees, 1992; Kozlowski and Hill, 1993). From this, attempts have been made to use environmental assessment methods as a means of developing human settlements in the form of sustainable cities (Breheny 1992a, 1992b; Breheny and Rookwood, 1993; Breheny, *et al.*, 1993; Breheny, 1995; Selman, 1996). This in turn has led to the development of methods that stress the need to assess whether-or-not the environmental capacity (ecological-integrity, equity, participation, and futurity) required to not only carry the city of tomorrow, but its cultural heritage in forms of sustainable human settlement, currently exists (Brandon, *et al.*, 1997).

Recent surveys of environmental assessment examine how the methods are currently being used. The examinations in question provide:

- reviews of how assessment methods are being drawn upon to promote sustainable development through resource conservation and environmental protection policies (Thrivel, 1992; Glasson, *et al.*, 1994; Jowsey and Kellnet, 1996; Lichfield, 1996);
- evaluations of the impact that major infrastructure and building installation projects have upon resource conservation, environmental protection and the sustainable development of cities (Guy and Marvin, 1997; Marvin and Guy, 1997; Brandon, *et al.*, 1997);
- meta-analysis' of the potential that assessment methods have to conserve resources, build environmental capacity, support the city of tomorrow and its cultural heritage in forms of sustainable human settlement (Bergh, *et al.*, 1997; Nijkamp and Pepping, 1998).

Such surveys illustrate that gaps exist between the inter-related activities of the urban life cycle, the assessment methods cover, and the sustainable development issues addressed by the analysis (Cooper, 1997). An example of this can be found in the different assessment techniques used in the EIA of larger urban development projects (i.e. infrastructure projects), and those drawn upon to assess individual building installations (Cooper and Curwell, 1998).

The surveys also reveal that scientific opinion concerning the potential of environmental assessment is currently divided. Firstly, there are those who are of the opinion that environmental assessment methods can be used to promote sustainable development (Brandon, *et al.*, 1997; Bergh, 1997; Nijkamp and Pepping, 1998). Secondly, there are others who are of the opinion that the all-pervasive marketisation, privatisation, resultant risk, and uncertainty surrounding the nature of public goods means that the methods of environmental assessment currently available are no longer appropriate. This division of opinion is important for two reasons. Firstly, it illustrates that the scientific community is divided about

Sustainable Urban Development 127

the value of assessment methods and, secondly, the division of opinion that tends to undermine the certainty the professional community needs to be confident about the worth of carrying out such assessments (Pugh, 1996; Cooper, 1997; 1999; Guy and Marvin, 1997).

The position of BEQUEST

The position taken by BEQUEST is aligned with the opinion that the scientific community is divided about the value of assessment methods because the networked community considers that environmental assessment methods can be used to promote sustainable urban development. In this respect the uncertainty and risk surrounding the process of privatisation represents a particular, but not insurmountable challenge for the scientific community. The source of such division lies in the absence of appropriate frameworks. Furthermore, a less than systematic approach that has previously been taken towards the inter-related activities of the urban life cycle, sustainable development issues, spatial levels, and time scales previously referred to (Curwell, *et al.*, 1998; Cooper and Curwell, 1998).

The assessment methodology adopted by the networked community is based upon an understanding that the growing international and increasingly global nature of the relationship between the environment and economy is uncertain. This can result in the, as yet, incalculable degrees of risk associated with EC policy and any actions taken by member states about resource conservation. This, in turn, means that standard methods of environmental valuation are of limited help in building the capacity needed to qualify if the city of tomorrow is able to carry its cultural heritage, and whether the forms of human settlement that develop from urban development are sustainable. Such assessments increasingly require the use of non-standard valuation (hedonic, and contingency type) methods (Powell *et al.*, 1997). Perhaps more critically, the networked community is of the opinion that standard and non-standard valuation methods are of limited use in assessing sustainable development because it is necessary to transcend such valuations as part of a co-evolutionary approach to environmental assessment. This is an approach that develops a holistic framework for the analysis of sustainable development and integrates the environmental, economic, and social elements as part of its assessment methodology (Facheaux, *et al.*, 1996; O'Conner, 1998; Facheaux and O'Conner, 1998). It is an approach that has a framework for analysis, which represents the development of environmental, economic, and social elements as complementary in the sense that environmental protection conserves resources, reduces depletion rates, and builds the capacity that the city of tomorrow to carry its cultural heritage. It is recognised that the capacity the city of tomorrow has to carry its cultural heritage in economic and social structures, which develop as forms of sustainable human settlement in terms of the quality of life they institute.

128   *Methodologies, Models and Instruments*

Transcending environmental valuation

It should perhaps also be noted that concern with the quality of life is significant because it transcends the issues of current concern to environmental valuation (property rights, landscape, recreation, and leisure). It is significant because its emphasis is upon the valuation of the environment in terms of ecosystem integrity (resource consumption, pollution, land use, and bio-diversity) and upon the scientific basis of such assessments. Their purpose is to turn attention towards the ecology of resource consumption. The advantage lies in the provision to develop environmental methods, which apply the so-called 'hard' certainties of biophysical science to the more uncertain and risky, social relations that are 'softer' and which are by nature more difficult to predict (Facheaux and O'Conner, 1998). This is achieved by emphasising the co-evolutionary nature of the biophysical and social elements in a framework that integrates them and which in turn provides the methodology for assessing the sustainability of development. This focuses attention on the hard and soft issues of sustainable development and how to integrate them into the methods adopted for such assessments (Fusco, *et al.*, 1997; Capello, *et al.*, 1999). In this instance, the issues are integrated in forms of environmental appraisal and impact assessments that provide statements on the sustainability of development. Environmental appraisals and impact assessments that transcend existing valuation techniques develop, in turn, as forms of sustainability assessments.

Transforming environmental assessment

The significance of such methods is their tendency to transcend existing valuation techniques, but transform environmental assessment *per se*. This is because forms of sustainability assessments go a long way towards transforming environmental assessment methodology into the post-Brundtland directory of environmental assessment methods needed, in this instance to:

- qualify if the capacity exists for the city of tomorrow is to carry its cultural heritage; and
- evaluate whether the economic and social structures underlying this process of urban development produce forms of human settlement that are sustainable.

The post-Brundtland directory

As a response, the partners of BEQUEST have sought to survey the methods currently in existence and to provide the networked community with a post-Brundtland directory of environmental assessment. The methods surveyed are classified in terms of the following: name, description, data required, status (well-

Sustainable Urban Development 129

established or experimental), activity (planning, design, construction, and operation), environmental and social issues (environmental, economic, social, and institutional), scale of assessment (spatial level, and time scale), and references. The survey has identified 64 methods available to conserve resources and build environmental capacity, including those methods that have been applied to the planning, design, construction, and operational activities of the urban life cycle.

The directory can be accessed via the web-site address referred to above. This provides a copy of each standard classification and, in a number of cases, offers hypertext links to the case studies they have been drawn from. Thus an opportunity is provided to explore the implications of applying the method in further detail and satisfying themselves as to whether the technique is appropriate for the assessment under consideration. The methods are drawn from a survey of the scientific literature and unpublished reports written by professional members of the community. In certain cases, they represent assessment methods that partners and extranet members of BEQUEST have been engaged in developing, or have a detailed knowledge.

The assessment methods

The assessment methods fall into two classes, 'environmental valuations', and those developing into particular forms of 'sustainability assessments'. The survey has found that post-Brundtland, environmental valuations tend to focus on assessments of eco-system integrity that develop into particular forms of sustainability assessments. These tend to focus on building the environmental capacity needed to not only qualify the integrity of eco-systems, but the equity, participation and futurity of the economic, social and institutional structures underlying the city of tomorrow and its cultural heritage.

Examples of the 'environmental valuation' class of methods include cost-benefit, hedonic, and multi-criteria analysis. The forms of sustainability assessments have been sub-classified as 'environmental appraisal' (simple base-line qualifications) and 'environmental impact assessments' (complex and advanced evaluations). In terms of the environmental valuations and forms of sustainability assessments, the methods tend to further sub-divide into the following types:

- those centring on the assessments of projects providing the infrastructures (energy, water and drainage, transport, telecommunication technologies, leisure and tourism) required to build the environmental capacity (ecological integrity, equity, participation and futurity) needed for the city of tomorrow to carry its cultural heritage (Banister and Burton, 1993; Nijkamp and Pepping, 1994; Graham and Marvin, 1996; William, *et al.*, 1996; Nijkamp, *et al.*, 1997; Guy and Marvin, 1997; Jones, *et al.*, 1996; Allwinkle and Speed, 1997).

130   *Methodologies, Models and Instruments*

- those assessment methods focussing on the procurement and installation of operations, qualification and evaluation of whether the forms of human settlement which it builds are sustainable (Prior, 1993; Vale and Vale, 1993; Cole, 1997; Curwell, *et al.*, 1999; Deakin, 1999).

Building environmental capacity

The survey of the assessment methods currently being used to conserve resources and build environmental capacity represents the classification of each method by inter-related activities of the urban life cycle. The sustainable development issues, spatial level, and time scale that both classes of assessment methods (environment valuations and forms of sustainability assessments are applied with the object of building environmental capacity.

Figure 11.2 maps the methods by the inter-related activities (planning, design, construction, and operation) of the urban life cycle, sustainable development issues, spatial level, and time scale of assessment and illustrates the strength of representation across the range of activities. In this aggregated form, the survey provides evidence to suggest that a wide range of methods exist to assess the environmental capacity of all activities. The purpose of mapping the assessment methods by such co-ordinates is fourfold. Firstly, it illustrates the range and spread of methods currently available. Secondly, it provides the means by which the assessment methods being used are identified. Thirdly, it identifies the strength of representation by sustainable development issue, spatial level, and time scale and, fourthly, it draws attention to the gaps that exist in the range and spread of methods needed to provide an integrated assessment of environmental capacity. It also provides the opportunity to direct further research aimed at developing the methodology (science, theory, and practice) of environmental assessment.

The mapping exercise suggests that the scientific and professional communities are drawing on assessment methods to build environmental capacity. It provides evidence to suggest the assessment methods that are being used to build environmental capacity (ecological integrity, equity, participation, and futurity) in the policy planning, infrastructure design, construction procurement, and operation of installations. Finally, it also illustrates that it is the urban life cycle, sustainable development issues, spatial levels, and time scales of the planning policy and infrastructure design activities that are the most strongly represented forms of assessment. This is largely because the other forms of assessment (construction and operation) are not as well covered in terms of sustainable development issues, spatial level, or time scale (see Figure 11.2). Thus, it suggests that the gaps in the range and spread of methods needed to provide an integrated assessment are located here in the construction and operation stages of the urban life cycle, their particular sustainable development issues, spatial levels, and time scales.

It should be noted that Figure 11.2 does not map how the assessment methods represent the ecological integrity, equity, participation, and futurity issues underlying the sustainability issues of the urban development process. To be more

Sustainable Urban Development   131

explicit, further analysis will need to be carried out to extend beyond the matrix-based mapping set out in Figure 11.2, and introduce a more comprehensive grid referencing system. Such a system could map, not only the urban development process in terms of its life cycle, sustainability, spatial levels and temporal scale, but cross-reference them with the ecological integrity, equity, participation and futurity components of the assessment methods in a form of 'frontier analysis'.

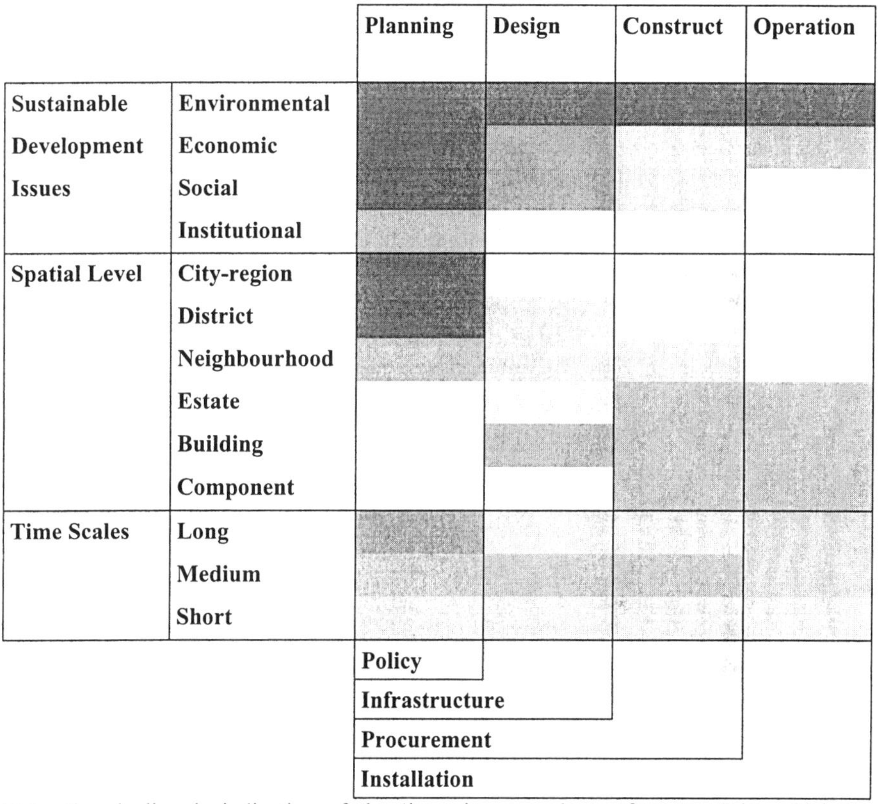

		Planning	Design	Construct	Operation
Sustainable Development Issues	Environmental				
	Economic				
	Social				
	Institutional				
Spatial Level	City-region				
	District				
	Neighbourhood				
	Estate				
	Building				
	Component				
Time Scales	Long				
	Medium				
	Short				
	Policy				
	Infrastructure				
	Procurement				
	Installation				

Note: the shading is indicative of the 'intensity scores', or 'frequency' by which the assessment methods address the sustainable urban development issues in question.

Figure 11.2   Assessment methods

Conclusions

This chapter has outlined the areas of the Environment and Climate Programme (Economic and Social Aspects of Human Settlement) that the BEQUEST project addresses. Furthermore, it has examined the framework it proposes for a common understanding of sustainable urban development and assessment methods currently

132   *Methodologies, Models and Instruments*

made use of by planners, architects, engineers, and surveyors to build environmental capacity by:

- fore-grounding the question of urban development and representing the process of urbanisation as a life cycle of inter-related activities;
- agreeing the sustainable development issues underlying the urban process; and
- identifying the environmental, economic and social structure, spatial level and time scales of sustainable urban development.

The chapter has then set out the issues that the BEQUEST project addresses in transcending environmental valuations, transforming assessment methodology, and moving towards a post-Brundtland directory of environmental assessment methods. This in tun has led to a classification of the environmental assessment methods contained in the directory. It has suggested that the methods fall into two classes, 'environmental valuations', and those developing into forms of 'sustainability assessments', and proposed that environment valuations tend to focus on assessments of eco-system integrity. Those methods that are augmenting into particular forms of sustainability assessment tend to focus on the environmental capacity that is needed to ensure both the integrity of eco-systems, and sustainable development of the economic, social and institutional structures underlying the city of tomorrow and its cultural heritage. Furthermore, it has suggested that such assessment methods are used to evaluate whether the forms of human settlement, which develop from this process of urban development, are sustainable in terms of the quality of life they offer. The chapter has also begun to highlight some of the current problems associated with the application of methods and weaknesses in the assessment of SUD, including:

- the need to extend the analysis beyond the matrix-based mapping and to introduce a more comprehensive grid referencing system, that can map, the urban development process in terms of its life cycle, sustainability, spatial levels, and temporal scale. Furthermore, it would cross-reference them with the ecological integrity, equity, participation, and futurity components of the assessment in a form of 'frontier analysis';
- the difficulty current assessment methods have in dealing with the complexity of institutional structures and associated stakeholder interests;
- the tendency for the policy planning and infrastructure design stages to overshadow the assessment needs of the other stages resulting in a situation where, comparatively speaking, relatively little is known about either the procurement of construction, or installation of operations;

Sustainable Urban Development 133

- the paucity of sustainable development indicators currently available in relation to a broader context of environmental, economic and social issues; and
- the problem of assessing the aggregate effect policy, infrastructure, procurement, and installations have upon attempts to build environmental capacity (ecological integrity, equity, public participation and futurity), and also to qualify and evaluate whether the city of tomorrow has a cultural heritage and pattern of human settlement that is sustainable.

Finally, it is recognised that methods able to overcome such difficulties are currently in the research phase and that practical tools for a fully integrated assessment of SUD are still some years away. In the meantime, the decision support toolkit being developed by BEQUEST will provide some assistance to professional actors. It will identify appropriate and relevant methods quickly and enable them to be linked together in order to establish whether the city of tomorrow and forms of human settlement, which evolve from the process of urban development, are sustainable.

References

Allwinkle, S. and Speed, C., 1997. Sustainability and the built environment: tourism impacts. In: Brandon P., Lombardi P. and Bentivegna V., (eds.), *Evaluation in the Built Environment for Sustainability*, E&FN Spon, London.

Banister, D. and Burton, K., 1993. *Transport, the Environment and Sustainable Development*, E&FN Spon, London.

Bentivenga, V., 1997. Limitations in environmental evaluations. In: Brandon P., Lombardi, P. and Bentivegna, V., (eds.), *Evaluation in the Built Environment for Sustainability*, E&FN Spon, London.

Bergh, J., Button, K., Nijkamp, P. and Pepping, G., 1997. *Meta-Analysis of Environmental Policies*, Klewer, Dordrecht.

Brandon, P., Lombardi, P. and Bentivenga, A., 1997. Introduction. In: Brandon, P., Lombardi, P. and Bentivegna, V., (eds.), *Evaluation of the Built Environment For Sustainability*, E&FN Spon, London.

Breheny, M., 1992a. The compact city, *Built Environment*, **18**(4).

Breheny, M., 1992b. *Sustainable Development and Urban Forms*, Pion, London.

Breheny, M., Gent, T. and Lock, D., 1993. *Alternative Development Patterns: New Settlements*, HMSO, London.

Breheny, M and Rookwood, R., 1993. Planning the sustainable city region. In: Blowers, A. (ed.), *Planning for a Sustainable Environment*, Earthscan Publications Ltd, London.

CEC, 1993. *Toward Sustainability*, Commission of the European Community, European's Fifth Environmental Action Programme, Brussels.

134   *Methodologies, Models and Instruments*

Capello R., Nijkamp P. and Pepping, G., 1999. *Sustainable Cities and Energy Policies*, Springer-Verlag, Berlin.

Cole, R., 1997. Prioritising environmental criteria in building design. In: Brandon, P., Lombardi, P. and Bentivegna, V., *Evaluation of the Built Environment for Sustainability*, E&FN Spon, London.

Cooper, I., 1997. Environmental assessment methods for use at the building and city scale: constructing bridges or identifying common ground. In: Brandon, P., Lombardi, P. and Bentivenga V., *Evaluation of the Built Environment for Sustainability*, E&FN Spon, London.

Cooper, I., 1999. Which focus for building assessment methods? *Building Research and Information*, **27**(4).

Cooper, I., 2000. Inadequate grounds for a 'design-led' approach to urban design, *Building Research and Information*, **28**(3).

Cooper, I. and Curwell, S., 1998. The implications of urban sustainability, *Building Research and Information*, **26**(1).

Curwell, S., Hamilton, A. and Cooper, I., 1998. The BEQUEST Network: towards sustainable urban development, *Building Research and Information*, **26**(1).

Curwell, S., Yates, A., Howard, N., Bordass, B. and Doggart, J., 1999. The Green Building Challenge in the UK, *Building Research and Information*, **27**(4/5).

Davoudi, S., 1997. Economic development and environmental gloss: a new structure plan for Lancashire. In: Brandon, P, Lombardi, P and Bentivenga, V, *Evaluation of the Built Environment for Sustainability*, E&FN Spon, London.

Deakin, M, 1996. Discounting, obsolescence, depreciation and their effects on the environment of cities, *Journal of Financial Management of Property and Construction*, **1**(2).

Deakin, M., 1997. An economic evaluation and appraisal of the effects land use, building obsolescence and depreciation have on the environment of cities. In: Brandon, P., Lombardi, P. and Bentivenga V., *Evaluation of the Built Environment for Sustainability*, E&FN Spon, London.

Deakin, M., 1999. Valuation, appraisal, discounting, obsolescence and depreciation: towards a life cycle analysis and impact assessment of their effects on the environment of cities, *International Journal of Life Cycle Assessment*, **4**(2).

Deakin, M., 2000. Developing sustainable communities in Edinburgh's South East Wedge, *Journal of Property Management*, **4**(4).

Deakin, M., 2001. Modelling the development of sustainable communities in Edinburgh's South East Wedge, *Planning Practice and Research*, **16**(3).

Faucheaux, S., Pearce, D. and Proops, J., 1997. Introduction. In: Faucheaux, S., Pearce, D. and Proops, J. (eds.), *Models of Sustainable Development*, Edward Elgar, Cheltenham.

Faucheaux, S. and O'Conner, M., 1998. Introduction. In: Faucheaux, S. and O'Conner, M. (eds.), *Valuation for Sustainable Development*, Edward Elgar, Cheltenham.

Fusco, L. and Nijkamp P., 1997. *Le Valutazioni per lo Sviluppo Sostenibile della Città e del Territorio,* Angeli, Milan.

Glasson, J., Therival, R. and Chadwick, A., 1994. *Environmental Impact Assessment*, University College, London.

Graham, S. and Marvin, S., 1996. *Telecommunications and the City*, Routledge, London.

Grillenzoni, M., Ragazzoni, G., Bazzani, G. and Canavari, M., 1997. Land planning and resource evaluation for public investments. In: Brandon, P., Lombardi, P. and Bentivegna V., *Evaluation of the Built Environment for Sustainability*, E&FN Spon, London.

Guy, S. and Marvin, S., 1997. Splintering networks: cities and technical networks in 1990s Britain, *Urban Studies*, **34**(2).

Jones, P., Vaughan, N., Cooke, P. and Sutcliffe, A., 1997. An energy and environmental prediction model for cities. In: Brandon, P., Lombardi, P. and Bentivegna V., *Evaluation of the Built Environment for Sustainability*, E&FN Spon, London.

Jowsey, E. and Kellett, J., 1996. Sustainability and methodologies of environmental assessment for cities. In: Pugh, C. (ed.), *Sustainability, the Environment and Urbanisation*, Earthscan Publications Ltd., London.

Kozlowski, J. and Hill, J., 1993. *Towards Planning for Sustainable Development: A Guide or the Ultimate Threshold Method*, Avebury, Aldershot.

Lombardi, P., 2000. A framework for understanding sustainability in the cultural built environment. In: Brandon, P.S., Lombardi, P. and Srinath, P. (eds.), *Cities and Sustainability. Sustaining our Cultural Heritage*, Conference Proceedings, Vishva Lekha Sarvodaya, Sri Lanka, (**4**), 1-25.

Lombardi, P., 2001. Responsibilities toward the coming generation forming a new creed, *Urban Design Studies*, **7**.

Marvin, S. and Guy, S., 1997. Infrastructure provision, development process and the co-production of environmental value, *Urban Studies*, **34**(4).

Lichfield, N., 1996. *Community Impact Evaluation*, University College London.

Massam, B., 1988. Multi-criteria decision making (Mcdm) techniques in planning, *Progress in Planning*, **30**.

May, A., Mitchell, G. and Kupiszewska, D., 1997. The development of the Leeds quantifiable city model. In: Brandon, P., Lombardi, P. and Bentivegna, V., (eds.), *Evaluation of the Built Environment For Sustainability*, E&FN Spon, London.

Mega, V., 1996 Our city, our future: towards sustainable development in European cities, *Environment and Urbanisation*, **8**(1).

Mitchell, G., 1996. Problems and fundamentals of indicators of sustainable development, *Sustainable Development*, **4**(1).

Mitchell, G., 1999. *A Geographical Perspective on the Development of Sustainable Urban Regions*, Earthscan, London.

Mitchell, G., May, A. and McDonald, A., 1995. PICABUE: a methodological framework for the development of indicators of sustainable development, *International Journal of Sustainable Development and(?) World Ecology*, **2**.

Nijkamp, P., 1991. *Urban Sustainability*, Gower, Aldershot.

Nijkamp, P. and Pepping, G., 1998. A meta-analytic evaluation of sustainable city initiatives, *Urban Studies*, **35**.

Nijkamp, P. and Perrels, A., 1994. *Sustainable Cities in Europe: A Comparative Analysis of Urban Energy and Environmental Policies*, Earthscan, London.

Nijkamp, P., Rietveld, P. and Voogd, H., 1990. *Multicriteria Evaluation in Physical Planning*, Elsevier, Amsterdam.

Norgaard, R. and Howarth, R., 1991. Sustainability and discounting the future. In: Costanza, R., (ed.), *Ecological Economics*, Columbia University Press.

O'Conner, M., 1998. Ecological-economic sustainability. In: Faucheaux, S. and O'Conner, M. (eds.), *Valuation for Sustainable Development*, Edward Elgar, Cheltenham.

Palmer, J., Cooper, I. and van der Vost, R. 1997, Mapping out fuzzy buzzwords - who sits where on sustainability and sustainable development, *Sustainable Development*, **5**(2).

Pearce, D. and Markanya, A., 1989. *Environmental Policy Benefits: Monetary Valuation*, OECD, Paris.

Pearce, D. and Turner, R., 1990. *Economic of Natural Resources and the Environment*, Harvester Wheatsheaf, Hemel Hempstead.

Pearce, D. and Warford, J., 1993. *World Without End: Economic, Environment and Sustainable Development*, Oxford University Press, Oxford.

Prior, J., 1993. *Building Research Establishment Environment Assessment Method, BREEAM, Version 1/93, New Offices*, Building Research Establishment Report.

Pugh, C., 1996. Sustainability and sustainable cities. In: Pugh, C., (ed.), *Sustainability, the environment and Urbanisation*, Earthscan Publications Ltd., London.

Rees, W., 1992. Ecological footprints and appropriated carrying capacity: what urban economics leaves out, *Environment and Urbanisation*, **4**(2).

Rydin, Y., 1992. Environmental impacts and the property market. In: Breheny, M, (ed.) *Sustainable Development and Urban Form*, Earthscan Publications Ltd, London.

Selman, P., 1996. *Local Sustainability*, Sage, London.

Therivel, R., 1992. *Strategic Environmental Assessment*, Earthscan Publications Ltd., London.

UNCED, 1992. *Earth Summit 92 (Agenda 21)*, United Nations Conference on Environment and Development, Regency Press, London.

Vale, B. and Vale, R., 1993. Building the sustainable environment. In: Blowers, A. (ed.) *Planning for a Sustainable Environment*, Earthscan Publications Ltd, London.

Voodg, H., 1983. *Multi-Criteria Evaluation for Urban and Regional Planning*, Pion, London.

WCED (Brundtland Commission), 1987. *Our Common Future*, United Nations, New York.

William P., Anderson, P. and Kanaroglou, E., 1996. Urban form, energy and the environment: a review of issues, evidence and policy, *Urban Studies*, **33**(1).

Chapter 12

Object Model for Temporal Changes in Geographical Information Systems

Abdul Adamu, Souhiel Khaddaj and Munir Morad

Introduction

The current GIS approaches of representing changes of geographical phenomena do not provide the ability to examine the complexities within the changes, in order to allow the integration of changes for different themes (e.g. transportation networks, infrastructure facilities, population etc.). This has become a major problem because a change in one theme may have adverse effect on the others, thereby risking the work of urban planners. This situation is exacerbated by the fact that no adequate data models are available which could efficiently represent detailed changes, showing the pattern of relationship among the themes, the cause of changes and result of the changes over time (Sui, 1998).

This paper aims to investigate the conceptual model that will represent the semantics to allow the continuity and pattern of changes of the geographical objects to be determined based on temporal relationships between the versions, events and the processes over a time period. This work is mainly concerned with object tracking and evolution of objects over time. Object tracking and evolution include not only attribute changes to homogenous objects, but also major changes that lead to object transformations such as splitting or merging. The beginning of this paper contains discussion about temporal GIS, object oriented approaches and related work. In the following sections, a new GIS model is presented and a case study of the model is illustrated. Finally, the conclusion of this investigation is presented in the last section.

Temporal GIS

The commonly used snapshot based approach of representing changes in GIS, does not provide the needed capabilities for detailed analysis of geographical phenomena (Langran, 1993). Recent research proposals have used temporal GIS and object oriented techniques to explicitly define the relationship between the events (or processes) and the objects over time. These include the triad model and the event-oriented model. Object oriented paradigm had been used in a number of techniques such as version management (Wachowicz, 1999), identity-based method (Hornsby and Egenhofer 2000) and image sequences (Bobick and Davis 2001) to identify patterns of change within the objects (Worboys, 1994; Yuan, 1997; Bian, 2000). The triad model (Peuquet and Qian 1996) is an integrated model and consists of three independent and interrelated domains (i.e. location, feature, and time). Event-oriented models have been a topic of investigation in the past decade (Frank, 1994; Peuquet and Duan, 1995; Claramunt *et al.*, 1999). In the Peuquet and Duan model all changes are time-stamped as a sequence of events through time. The changes are time-stamped and stored in increasing order from the initial event. Frank represented an ordinal model where events (not time-stamped) are linked in sequential order. Claramunt and Theriault (1996) investigation describes object changes in the past, present and future.

Object oriented model for GIS

Although, the triad model represents an integrated approach for representing changes, it does not relate events to the geographical phenomena. The event-oriented model represents events which are suitable for temporal stable changes but are not suitable for representing sudden changes (i.e. earthquake) and gradual changes (i.e. rainfall) (Peuquet, 1998). The Claramunt and Theriault model represents the events related to the change but stores the changes as attributes of the object and the model is not suitable for tracking the evolution of the geographical objects involving splitting, merging, or transition.

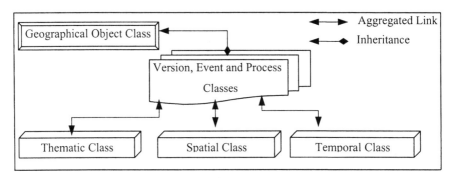

Figure 12.1 Composite classes of a geographical object

The proposed model is based on object oriented techniques and it will be referred to as the Object Oriented model for GIS (OOGIS). The OOGIS model supports both object and attributes versioning. According to the OOGIS model, version management handles changes of geographical phenomena. A version of the object consists of composite classes as in Figure 12.1. The aggregated composite classes include thematic class, spatial class, and temporal class. The associated composite classes include events class and processes class. The spatial class deals with queries about the location of the object (e.g. where is the best museum in this city?). The thematic class deals with queries about the features of an object (e.g. what is the highest building, or what is the speed limit of this road?). The temporal class deals with the queries about the time attributes of the object (e.g. when was the first hospital built in London?). Furthermore, an event class deals with the cause of the changes of the geographical object (e.g. why did they reduce the speed limit of this road?). And, a process class deals with effect of the changes of the object (e.g. how much of this rain will cause a flood?).

The versions class

A geographical object is represented as generic object, the first object and any subsequent changes can be represented as versions. Each version of the object consists of changes (involving an attribute or behaviour) of the aggregated classes (spatial, thematic, and temporal) and the associated class (events and processes). Subsequent changes of attributes of the versions will generate related dynamic attributes and temporal links to be updated to the respective versions (Owen, 1993). The relationships between the generic object and the versions of the object are represented by a temporal version management approach (Dadam *et al.*, 1984; Wachowicz, 1999). The version management uses temporal operators (e.g. during, after, before etc.) to handle gradual and sudden changes (Allen, 1984; Al-Taha, 1992). As shown in Figure 12.2, simple (linear) geographical phenomenon (involving changes in attributes) and complex phenomenon (involving splitting and merging of objects) were investigated using this model.

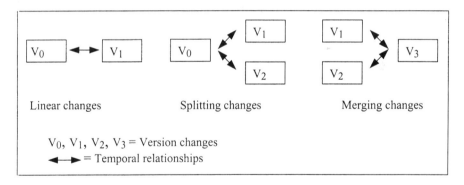

Figure 12.2 Types of real world activities experienced by geographical objects

To avoid the use of large storage space, only the generic object or the current object holds the complete attributes and behaviour of the object whiles the other versions represents the changes of their attributes and behaviour.

The temporal relationships between current object and versions can be verified by equation (1):

$$Versions(x) = (\,_x(n,n_0),\,_x(n-1,n_0),....,\,_x(n_0+1,\,n_0), CV_x(n_0)) \tag{1}$$

where $CV_x(n)$ stands for the complete version number n of the object x whiles n_0 indicates the generic version. The changes between the current version (k) and the previous version (k') are represented by delta, $\Delta_x(k, k')$. As shown in equation (1), the current versions are derived from the previous versions and this strategy is referred to as forward based versioning. All the versions are related to the basic version n_0, hence any of the versions can be accessed at equal time. The delta value remained the same when new version is created. As shown in equation (2), previous versions can be evaluated from current versions and this strategy is known as the backward based versioning. The method in equation (2) provides a quicker access to the current versions.

$$Versions(x) = (CV_x(n), \Delta_x(n, n-1), \Delta_x(n-1, n-2), ..., \Delta_x(n_0+1, n_0)) \qquad (2)$$

Spatial, thematic and temporal classes

As shown in Figure 12.3, the relationships between the attribute and behaviour changes improve the efficiency of the query mechanism of the OOGIS model and reduce the data access time. They record only the attribute or behaviour changes to minimise redundancy and data storage. To promote detailed and continuous analysis of the changes, there are relationships (bi-directional) between the changes (attributes and behaviour) of each version.

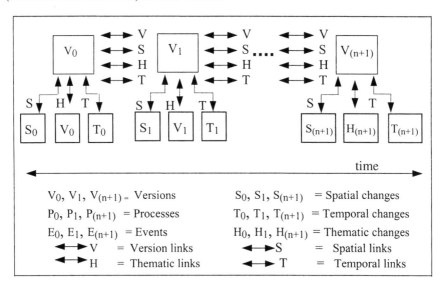

Figure 12.3 Relationships between the attributes and behaviours changes of the spatial classes of the versions of the object

Events and processes classes

The event class has an initial associations link with the version class. Subsequent association links between the event class and the version class are produced through the bi-directional links. Recording of events is time-stamped as both absolute time and relative time, in order to be able to deal with known dates of events; but the recording can also be sequential using temporal relationships to determine unknown dates of events. The recording of the attributes of the events (e.g. starting time, ending time, speed, position etc.) enables the OOGIS model to deal with sudden changes (such as earthquake) as well as gradual changes (such as rainfall). As shown in Figure 12.4, there are temporal relationships between the events to improve the efficiency of the systems. The processes have attributes such as start time and end time to be able to handle sudden changes (such as structure damage) as well as gradual changes (such as urban flooding).

The relationship between the versions of a geographical object, the events, and processes is shown in Figure 12.4. There are no direct association relationships between the event class and the process class. The relationship between the event class and process class is through the version class.

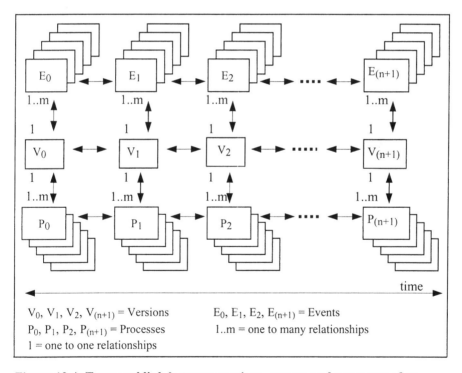

Figure 12.4 Temporal link between versions, events, and processes of an object

A case study

This case study of the OOGIS model involves a special dataset, consisting of changes of geographical phenomena over four time frames during the period from 1850 to 2000. The studied changes are shown in Figure 12.5a, 12.5b, 12.5c, and 12.5d. In 1850, grassland (labelled 1) in Figure 12.5a, experienced non-homogenous changes due to shortage of rain and sunshine conditions. In 1900, it was recorded that some sections of grassland were barren (labelled 4) while some sections of grassland remained the same (labelled 1) in Figure 12.5b. Further on in 1950, it was noted the whole space occupied by the barren land and grassland, as in Figure 12.5c, had been flooded (labelled 6). As indicated in Figure 12.5d, the flood land was eventually turned into an airport site (labelled 9) in 2000, as the population around the area increased.

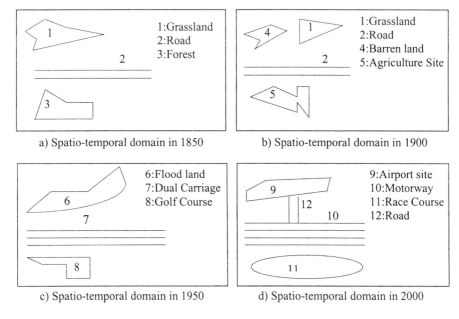

Figure 12.5 Case Study

The relationships between the events and processes as shown in Figure 12.6 allow the tracking of the respective versions of the attributes and behaviour over time. For example, the spatial attributes and behaviour of the grass land (V_0) are linked to the spatial attributes and behaviour of the barren land (V_1) and the grass land (V_2). The barren land (V_1) and grassland (V_2) are linked with the flood land (V_3). The flood land (V_3) is linked with the airport land (V_4). As shown in Figure 12.7, the relationships between attributes and behaviour promote continuous backward and forward movement through the versions of the object.

Object Model for Temporal Changes in GIS   143

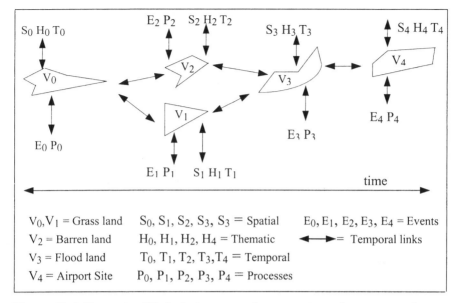

Figure 12.6 Example of links between versions, events, and processes of geographical changes

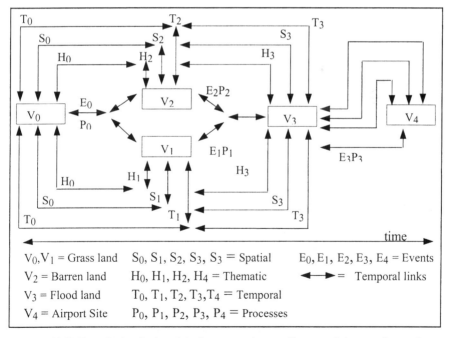

Figure 12.7 Detailed relationship between the attributes of the versions, the events and processes of the geographical object

Conclusion

Different approaches to representing changes of geographical phenomena for analysing and tracking the evolution of objects have been discussed, many of which have not been successfully implemented. The models did not take into account the evolution (e.g. splitting, transformation etc.) of a specific object, which can involve more than changes to its attributes and effect the changes has on other geographical objects. The OOGIS model proposed here tackles the limitations of previous work and provides an integrated framework for effective tracking of the evolution of the geographical object. The OOGIS model deals with gradual and sudden changes because attributes of the events have temporal operators and events of the versions have relationships between them. Also, less data storage will be required when implementing OOGIS model since only the changes of the object are represented as versions, which will be carried out in future works.

References

Allen, J., F., 1984. Towards a general theory of action and time, *Artificial Intelligence*, **23**, 123-154.

Al-Taha, K., 1992. *Temporal Reasoning in Cadastral Systems*. PhD thesis, Department of Surveying Engineering, University of Maine, Orono, ME.

Bian, L., 2000. Object-oriented representation for modelling mobile objects in an aquatic environment, *International Journal of Geographical Information Science*, **14**(7), 603-623.

Bobick, A.F. and Davis, J.W., 2001. The recognition of human movement using temporal templates, *IEEE Transaction on Pattern and Machine Intelligence*, **23**(3), 257-267.

Claramunt, C. and Theriault, M., 1996. Towards semantics for modelling spatio-temporal processes within GIS, *7th International Symposium on Spatial Data Handling*, SDH'96, August, 12-16.

Claramunt, C., Parent, C., Spaccapietra, S. and Theriault, M., 1999. Database Modelling for Environmental and Land Use Changes. In: Stillwell, J., Geertman, S. and Openshaw, S. (eds.), *Geographical Information and Planning*, 182-202.

Dadam, P., Lum, V. and Werner, H.D., 1984. Integrating of time versions into relational database systems, *Proceeding of the Conference on Very Large Database*, 509-522.

Frank, A., 1994. Qualitative temporal reasoning in GIS ordered time scales, *Sixth International Symposium on Spatial Data Handling*, Edinburgh, Scotland, International Geographical Union, 410-30.

Hornsby, K. and Egenhofer, M., 2000. Identity-based change: a foundation for spatio-temporal knowledge representation, *International Journal of Geographical Information Science*, **14**(3), 207-224.

Langran, G., 1993. Manipulation and analysis of temporal GIS, *Proceedings of the Canadian Conference on GIS*, Canada, 869-879.

Owen, P.K., 1993. Dynamic functions triggers in an on-line topology environment, *European Conference on Geographical Information Systems (EGIS)*, **2**, 1249-1255.

Peuquet, D., 1998. *Time in GIS and geographical databases*. In: Longley, P., Goodchild, M., Maguire, D. and Rhind, D. (eds.), *Geographical Information Systems: Principles and Ttechnical Issues. Volume 1.*

Peuquet, D. and Duan, N., 1995. An event-based spatio-temporal data model (ESTDM) for temporal analysis of geographical data, *International Journal of Geographical Information Systems*, **9**(1), 7-24.

Peuquet, D.L. and Qian, 1996. An integrated database design for temporal GIS. In: M., Kraak, M. and Molenaar, M. (eds.), *Spatio-temporal I; Spatio-Temporal Data I in Advances in GIS Research*.

Sui, D.Z., 1998. GIS-based urban modelling practices, problems, and prospects, *International Journal of Geographical Information Systems*, **8**, 7-24.

Wachowicz, M., 1999. *Object-Oriented Design for Temporal GIS*, Taylor and Francis, London.

Worboys, M., 1994. Object-oriented approaches to geo-referenced information, *International Journal of Geographical Information Systems*, **6**, 353-399.

Yourdon, E., 1994. *Object-Oriented System Design: an Integrated Approach*, Yourdon Press.

Yuan, M., 1997. *An Intelligent GIS to support spatiotemporal modeling in Hydrology.* http://ncgia.ucgia.edu/conf/SANTA_FE_CD-ROM/sf_paper/yuan_may/may.html.

Chapter 13

Using GIS Techniques to Evaluate Community Sustainability in Open Forestlands in Sub-Saharan Africa

Yang Li, Alan Grainger, Zoltan Hesley, Ole Hofstad, Prem Lal Sankhayan,
Ousmane Diallo and Aku O'Kting'Ati

Introduction

The sustainable development of humanity is inextricably linked with how well it manages its impacts on natural resources and the environment. For many people in developed countries this is an attractive concept but a rather abstract one, because:

- they are very remote from the sources of the natural resources on which they depend;
- they are just as content with human-made urban environments as with natural rural environments; and
- their societies contain many possible mechanisms to substitute for natural resources that become scarce.

For many people in developing countries, on the other hand, the situation is very different. The sustainability of their livelihoods fundamentally depends on a day-to-day basis on the ability of their local environments to sustain supplies of food, wood, and animal forage. They lack the substitution mechanisms that operate on a national scale in developed countries, and their relationships with natural resources and the environment are much more spatially focused. If stocks of natural resources around a village become depleted and/or its local environment becomes degraded then it may cease to be sustainable, forcing its inhabitants to move somewhere else.

Community sustainability in villages in developing countries is therefore not an abstract notion but very real, and so is highly suitable for evaluation. This chapter describes how models can be used to give insights into the sustainability of villages in three African countries, Senegal, Tanzania, and Uganda, and to form the

Using GIS to Evaluate Community Sustainability   147

basis for planning techniques. The villages are all situated in areas of open forests, and so their sustainability also depends on being resilient to frequent droughts.

The key difficulty in evaluating sustainability in these settings derives from the fact that open forests contain multiple vegetation layers, which are spatially heterogeneous and used by many people for many different purposes. This problem is made tractable here by integrating two types of models:

- classic optimisation models that use linear programming techniques to balance multiple uses within certain constraints; and
- Geographic Information System (GIS) models that allow the:

> capturing, storing, checking, integrating, manipulating, analysing and display of data which are spatially referenced to the Earth (Department of Environment, 1987)

and, which are therefore highly suited to representing both complex spatial distributions of resources and spatio-temporal changes in them.

Different approaches to land use planning and evaluation

It is important at the outset to acknowledge that different approaches are taken to land use planning and evaluation, and that the approach required for modelling may differ from that used by local people.

The rational approach

In a rational approach, the sustainability of every area on the planet would be assured if it were used according to its suitability for particular uses, determined by the land's natural capability, as enhanced by artificial inputs. If an area is suited to a range of land uses, referring to economic criteria will make a rational choice. Everyone will at any time have perfect information about the potential uses of every area and the markets for goods, which may be produced from it. They will also care about the long-term sustainability of their livelihoods and tolerate no action that would prejudice this.

The behavioural approach

In a behavioural approach, on the other hand, life is not so mathematically or economically perfect. Land uses will have developed iteratively in each area, in the absence of perfect information. Some areas will therefore still be used for purposes for which they are not ideally suitable, other areas will be overused in relation to the intensity of a suitable use, and still other areas that are potentially highly productive will not be used at all. Land use will also be influenced by other factors.

148   *Methodologies, Models and Instruments*

For example, the size of a herd may far exceed the notional carrying capacity of the rangelands to which a pastoralist has access, because:

- additional animals are kept to reflect ties with another family; or
- there is the perception that the larger the herd, the greater the chance that some animals will survive when drought strikes and forage production declines.

Furthermore, people will choose not to maximise profitability if this detracts from other objectives, such as leisure time, and will be satisfied with less demanding criteria than economic ones alone. Nor will there be the same obsession with the distant future, as survival will be perceived on a much shorter time period, in some cases even from day to day.

The role of Geographical Information Systems in evaluation

Rational evaluation using multiple data layers

Over the last twenty years, many new techniques have been developed in computer-based geo-information science that offer improved scope for spatial data collection, manipulation, visualisation, analysis and data quality management (Openshaw and Abrahart, 2000; Kidner and Higgs, 2001). GIS techniques have become increasingly popular for studying the spatial relationships between different natural and human attributes, and allowing the manipulation of multiple spatial datasets in quite sophisticated ways. This approach sits firmly within the rational approach to evaluation, described above. GIS techniques can be used to assess, far more quickly than a human being and more accurately, the multiple interactions between multiple data layers that are the basis of land use evaluation and planning.

Dynamic modelling

Besides manipulating contemporaneous spatial attributes, GIS can be used to simulate possible changes in attributes over time. Most GIS software still has quite limited dynamic capabilities, and so modelling spatio-temporal change requires, as in this case, that it be interfaced with other mathematical models. The use of such hybrid models is a fast developing field (Goodchild *et al.*, 1996).

Different pictures of the World

Every image potentially has great power, whether it is a computer image or the logo of a well-known commercial product. Once a map of a particular area or place has been produced using a computer it can assume a near unchallengeable status, however good its actual quality may be. Of course, in reality every map only represents only one view of an area and virtually every inhabitant of that area will have a different mental picture of it. Consequently, while maps produced using GIS techniques can be very beneficial, they can be as much a hindrance to reaching a consensus evaluation as a help.

Different perceptions of GIS products

The products of GIS operations may also be perceived in different ways by different people. Leading politicians and bureaucrats in developing countries, for example, might see GIS products as positive because they are characteristic of a technologically and economically advanced society. Other people might view them in a negative way because they are associated with 'experts', 'outsiders', and 'foreigners' and generally with external interference in their livelihoods.

Open forests and their modification

Open forests

Tropical open forests are forests comprising mixtures of trees, shrubs, and grasses in which the tree canopies do not form a continuous closed cover. They occur in savanna environments in the semi-arid, sub-humid and humid tropics. Savannas are usually portrayed as ecosystems containing trees but dominated by grasses (Adams, 1996), but they can also be classed as forests owing to their tree component (Lanly, 1982). Various combinations of climatic and edaphic factors and considerable human modification have given rise to a dispersed horizontal structure and discontinuous tree canopy cover which distinguishes open forests from closed forests - such as tropical rain forests - whose tree crowns almost completely cover the ground. Lanly (1982) used ecological criteria, not a critical value of percentage canopy cover, to separate open forest from closed forest.

Deforestation

The most drastic human impact on tropical rain forest is deforestation, defined here as:

> the temporary or permanent clearance of forest for agriculture or other purposes (Grainger, 1993).

If forest is not cleared, deforestation does not take place.

Forest degradation

Deforestation is clearly an inadequate term to represent the effects of impacts, which merely modify forest cover, whether or not clearance is involved. The term now widely used for this purpose is forest degradation, defined as a:

> temporary or permanent reduction in the density, structure, species composition or productivity of vegetation cover (Grainger, 1993).

Deforestation is an extreme case of degradation, as it temporarily reduces the density of vegetation cover to zero.

The wider context of land degradation

Land degradation is often associated only with soil degradation (Chisholm and Dumsday, 1987), but vegetation degradation also plays a prominent role, even in dry and sparsely vegetated parts of the tropics, where the degradation of soil and vegetation are the two main components of desertification (Grainger, 1992).

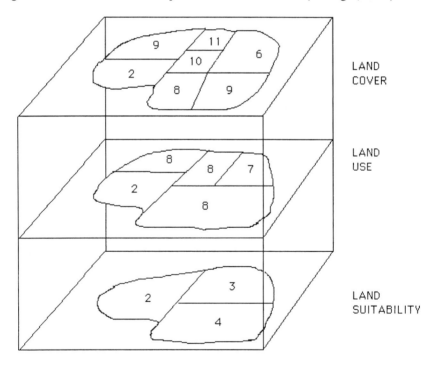

Figure 13.1 GIS model of an area of land by three layers of attributes: land suitability, land use, and land cover

Degradation: objective or pejorative?

Degradation is commonly perceived to be a 'bad' thing, and this is certainly encouraged by its association with desertification. However, given that deforestation is inevitable in the course of development, that most deforested countries do not think of themselves as being environmentally deprived, and that degradation is a much lesser impact than deforestation, it is right to challenge this perception. The term degradation is therefore used here in a strictly objective sense, to describe an environmental change, resulting from human impacts, that may reduce the environmental quality of an area while at the same time having the potential to be economically beneficial.

Open forestlands: tackling the modelling challenge

Assessing the sustainability of communities in open forestlands represents a tremendous challenge. Data on the distribution and composition of open forests is generally poor, since they have long been neglected in forest surveys, but both characteristics are known to be highly spatially variable. They are also subjected to a complex mixture of human impacts, in which multiple users simultaneously and/or sequentially exploit one or more of the vegetation layers - trees, bushes, and grass - for multiple uses. The tree and bush layers may decline in area (deforestation) at the same time as the remaining woody areas decline in biomass density, canopy cover and plant density (degradation).

Representing open forests by a GIS model

To tackle this challenge we first used a typical GIS strategy in which the features of a complex spatial phenomenon are disaggregated into various sets of discrete attributes. In this case the relevant attributes of each area of open forestland were grouped into three broad categories (Figure 13.1) of land suitability, land use, and land cover.

Each category was represented as a separate data layer, and further divided into multiple types, listed in Tables 13.1-13.3. Applying this classification divided the territory exploited by each village into mosaics of homogeneous areas of land suitability (Land Suitability Polygons, or LSPs), land use (Land Use Polygons, or LUPs) and land cover (Land Cover Polygons, or LCPs).

Each area of land with a land cover of open forest (of which more than one type was recognised (see Table 13.3) was characterised by a vertical structure of three vegetation layers: trees, bushes, and grass. Finally, each of these layers in turn was characterised by three interlinked sets of attributes: biomass density, plant density, and canopy cover.

This resulted in the hierarchy of degradation indicators shown in Figure 13.2. By simplifying the representation of open forestlands this procedure makes human impacts on them more amenable to modelling. The representation itself may be called, for convenience, the GIS Model.

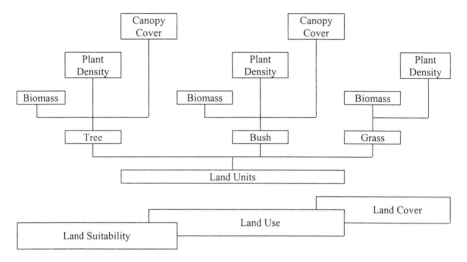

Figure 13.2 The hierarchy of open forest degradation indicators

Table 13.1 Land suitability classification system and code

1	Arable: rice cultivation
2	Arable: highest dryland grade (accommodates ploughing)
3	Moderately suitable for cultivation
4	Livestock raising and conservative cultivation
5	Grazing or tree plantations only
6	Conservative/nomadic grazing
7	Woodland management only. Unsuited to cropping or grazing
8	Unsuited to any use (conservation only)

Table 13.2 Land use classification system and code

1	Rice cultivation
2	Annual crops (ploughing)
3	Other annual crops (hoeing)
4	Annual crops mixed with trees
5	Perennial crops
6	Fallow
7	Pasture/grassland
8	Forest or woodland
9	No use

Table 13.3 Land cover classification and code

1	Cropland
2	Dense garden
3	Open garden
4	Dense fallow
5	Sparse fallow
6	Grassland
7	Open shrubland
8	Savanna
9	Woody savanna
10	Degraded savanna
11	Forest plantation/closed forest
12	Bare land or rock
13	Wetland

An optimisation model of multiple uses

Exploitation of open forestland by the members of the community, which depends on it, was then modelled using a dynamic linear programming model, the Dynamic Woodland Degradation (DWD) Model, coded in GAMS software. It allocated open forest resources around a village to supply local and non-local demand for food, forage, and fuel wood in an economically optimal way and predicted the resulting deforestation and forest degradation patterns. Resources were allocated iteratively on an annual basis over a 20-year period (2000-2020). All households were assumed in the model to first satisfy their basic needs for food, fuel, fodder etc. and only then did they maximise the present value of their joint income, using an annual discount rate of 15%. A village was assumed to have the social control mechanisms and central authority needed to maximise collective welfare and optimally allocate the village labour force. The main output of the model was the biomass density of each vegetation layer (trees, bushes and grass), although this was converted into equivalent outputs of tree and bush density and percent crown cover (Sankhayan and Hofstad, 2001).

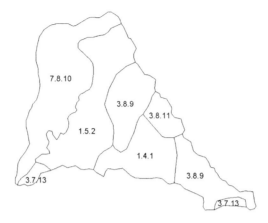

Figure 13.3 The concept of the land unit
An imaginary village with two LSPs and four LUPs. LSP 1 is suited to rice cultivation (n=1) and LSP 2 is moderately suited to cultivation (n=3). LUP 1 is cultivated for rice (n=1), LUP 2 for other annual crops (n=3), LUP 3 is pasture (n=7) and LUP 4 is woodland (n=8). Combinations of LSPs, LUPs and LCPs give a variety of Land Units (e.g. 1.1.1 is suitable for rice, cultivated for rice, and its land cover is cropland).

A stratagem to link GIS and environmental models

The DWD Model (Figure 13.3) had to be designed in such a way that the dynamic changes it predicted could be fully represented in spatial form, even though it had only a limited spatial capability and could not map distributions of LSPs, LUPs and LCPs separately. The solution was to divide each village territory into a set of 'mini-polygons', called Land Units, which are the smallest possible polygon division. Thus, Land Unit 3.8.9 is the part of LSP 3 ('moderately suitable for cultivation') covered by LUP 8 ('woodland') and LCP 9 ('woody savanna').

Modelling spatial change with a GIS degradation model

The DWD Model was linked to the GIS Model through an interface program, written in C and SPANS macros. Simulations with the combined GIS Degradation Model showed two main types of spatio-temporal changes in the sets of attributes of each area as follows:

- each type of land use could expand at the expense of another, as required to meet local demand. Typically, an area of cropland expanded into an area of open forest. Since in open forestlands some farmers merely clear a few trees and crop amongst the remaining ones we allowed for both full clearance (deforestation) and partial clearance (degradation). Cropland expansion occurred in Land Units that were (a) most suited to cropping and (b) closest to the village centre. It was assumed that shrinkage of open forest in a particular land unit is homogeneous along the boundary between it and the cropland land unit, which was expanding into it. This expansion was modelled using a one-dimensional buffer program written in SPANS macros; and

- the biomass of each of the three vegetation layers of open forestland could also decline (or rise), depending on the balance between harvests of fuel wood and forage, and vegetation regeneration. A net decline would constitute degradation, as defined above. Degradation by grazing and fuel wood cutting was assumed to be uniform over a land unit and its expansion also minimised travel distance. Withdrawals from tree, bush and grass layers of open forest were accounted for separately.

Modelling interactions between data layers

Separating the qualities of land into different attribute layers gives the potential to model interactions between them. In the present version of the model, the land cover of an area changes as its land use changes. However, land use could only change within limits set by land suitability, and so a cropping LUP could only expand into an area designated by an LSP as suitable for cropping. In future versions of the model we hope to relax this constraint to represent more realistic situations in which land is converted to uses for which it is not sustainable, thereby exacerbating soil and vegetation degradation.

Integration of multiple data sources

GIS was used as a hub in this research since it can integrate, visualise, handle, and analyse data from a range of different sources. Different GIS software products were used to take advantage of their specific functions at different stages of the project. Thus, the base maps were either scanned from paper maps to give TIFF files and then subjected to computer assisted vectorisation with ARC/Scan, or, in the case of field survey maps, digitised manually. The relevant boundaries were set with GPS data collected in the field. PCI SPANS was used as the primary spatial modelling environment, as it can handle both vector and raster data (aggregated as quadtrees), has strong data conversion functionality, and has files that are relatively simple and flexible. ARC/View was used to display SPANS output maps in a user-friendly, Windows environment.

The use of a diverse set of techniques in this research led to a requirement for an equally wide range of data sources (Figure 13.4). Base maps relied on field data supported by GPS data. Spatio-temporal simulations relied on output from the DWD Model, converted from a large binary file to a text file by a set of tools developed with Unix C Shell and SPANS macros. Data were then categorised according to different attributes, which were further separated by land unit. A series of attribute files were created for each biological specification of each land unit. The data were then regrouped and converted into SPANS table files. Another part of the project, not reported here, used maps classified from Landsat TM satellite images in ERDAS Imagine format, but converted into SPANS raster files to facilitate integration into the geo-information system. All these data had different formats, resolutions, classifications, and qualities. As the different software technologies viewed the same objects from different perspectives, integration was not straightforward (Ahlqvist, 2000), though there was sufficient overlap to make it feasible.

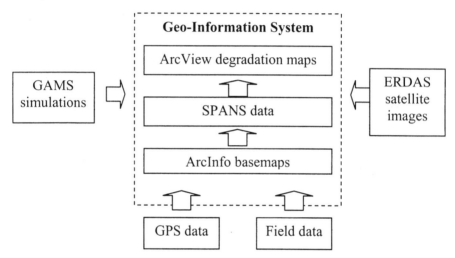

Figure 13.4 Integration of multiple data sources

Applying the model in Senegal, Tanzania, and Uganda

Study areas

Fourteen villages in Senegal, Tanzania, and Uganda were chosen as study sites to represent the range of climate, ecology, and land utilisation of open forestlands (Table 13.4). They were situated in the Department of Velingara in Senegal; three districts in Tanzania: Bagamoyo District, Handeni District, and Turiani District; and Nakasongola District in Uganda.

Data collection and production of village maps

In every village, structured interviews of village leaders and individual villagers were undertaken to collect data on (a) time allocation in farming, grazing and fuel wood collection, (b) household consumption and expenditure; (c) demand for food and fuel wood; and (d) other key elements of farming practices and open forest exploitation.

Figure 13.5 A map of Sare Coly Salle, Senegal

Villagers also helped to prepare a map of (a) the Legal Boundary of their village; (b) the Effective Boundary of their land use; and (c) the distribution of land use, land suitability, and vegetation cover. Each territory was divided into homogeneous Land Units in these three categories (Figure 13.5). Village and Land Unit boundaries were both mapped using a Global Positioning System (GPS) instrument.

Modelling deforestation

While the final outputs of the simulations combine both deforestation and degradation, Figure 13.6 shows an example of deforestation alone for the Senegalese village of Sare Coly Salle. Between 2000 and 2020 the large cropland land unit in the middle of the village territory clearly expands westward into the savanna land unit. There is also a slight expansion into the sparse fallow area in the east of the territory, though to compensate for this some of the adjacent savanna area is converted to fallow land.

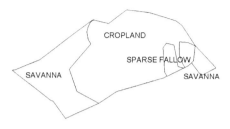

year 2000

year 2010

year 2020

Figure 13.6 Predicted trends in deforestation in Sare Coly Salle, Senegal between 2000-2020

Using GIS to Evaluate Community Sustainability 159

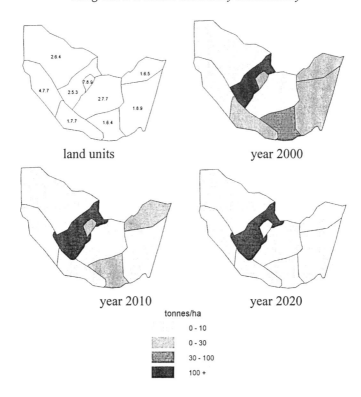

Figure 13.7 Trends in deforestation and open forest degradation (expressed as changes in tree biomass density) in Mazizi, Tanzania

Modelling deforestation and degradation

An example of a simulation of spatio-temporal trends in both deforestation and degradation is provided for the Tanzanian village of Mazizi, located in Bagamoyo District, illustrated in Figure 13.7. It has a moderate population density, high livestock density, and produces charcoal. The population is currently growing at 2.4% per annum. The proportion of territory cultivated in the year 2000 was less than 20%. The model predicted substantial degradation over the period 2000 to 2020, with an 80% fall in tree biomass density. The expansion of agriculture area (i.e. in land unit 2.5.3) is also obvious from the reduction in the area of open-shrublands adjacent to land unit 2.5.3.

160   *Methodologies, Models and Instruments*

Sustainability assessments

The model can be used in two ways to evaluate the long-term sustainability of open forestland use.

Indications from initialisation

Firstly, it can serve as a simple static accounting model to represent the sum of all impacts, of all members of a village community, on the lands within their territory at the start of the simulation period. For two of the Ugandan villages studied we found that even in 2000 the livelihoods of villagers could not be sustained by resources within the boundaries of the territory which they had defined for us. The only way to explain this problem was that villagers also illegally exploit wood and forage in a neighbouring State Forest Reserve. Naturally, they were not happy to admit this to outsiders.

Table 13.4   Summary Results of Simulations for 2000-2020

	Deforestation	**(%)**	**Degradation**	**(%)**
Senegal	Low	5	Moderate	25
Afia M'Bemba	No	0	Low	7
Boulimbou	Low	1	Moderate	15
Lambatara	Low	1	Low	8
Medina Pakane	Moderate	15	High	94
Sare Coly Salle	Low	7	Moderate	29
Sare M'Biro				
Tanzania				
Mazizi	Moderate	30	High	80
Kihangaiko Madesa	Moderate	26	Low	4
Kanga	Low	5	Moderate	18
Kilimanjaro	Low	3	High	97
Muungano	Low	6	Low	3
Kwadudu	Low	0	Moderate	19
Uganda				
Kyankonwa	Moderate	20	High	94
Namusala	Low	4	High	98

Indications from modelling long term trends in degradation

Most of the villages we studied in Senegal and Tanzania should be able to sustain themselves indefinitely using the open forestland resources within their territories,

Using GIS to Evaluate Community Sustainability 161

for while open forests were cleared and degraded during the 20-year simulation period the overall impact was relatively small. However, there was concern that Sare Coly Salle and Mazizi, both of which were predicted to experience moderate deforestation and high degradation (over 90%), and Kilimanjaro (also predicted to incur 90% degradation) would not be sustainable in the long term (Table 13.4).

In many of the villages studied relatively little deforestation was predicted, not because population growth was limited but because so little land was suitable for cropping but still unused. Consequently, while our model was able to simulate trends in deforestation and degradation si::ultaneously, it also showed that degradation could occur when villages encounter upper limits on cropland expansion.

Planning applications

Until now the emphasis of this paper has been on the external evaluation of community sustainability using the power of advanced technology. Is it possible that the same methods could also form the basis of tools that could be used by the villagers themselves?

A village resource inventory model

The same procedure used to construct the GIS Model of each village could be adapted so that villagers could assess the resources available to them as woodland, grazing land and cropland, and the potential for using these resources in a sustainable manner. They would first need to map the legal and effective boundaries of their village, and then divide whichever one of the corresponding territories was the largest into homogeneous areas of land suitability, current land use(s), and current land cover. They would then need to draw separate maps to show the distribution of tenurial rights, together with the location of any existing or potential conflicts between different land uses and/or land users (e.g. between farmers and nomadic pastoralists).

In our study these maps were digitised and then superimposed on a computer using GIS software. But superimposition could be achieved far more simply for village purposes by using pencils and tracing paper instead, or felt-tip pens and an overhead projector if these were available. Both options would permit easy comparison, and easy modification of the maps to show alternative scenarios.

A village land-use planning model

A more sophisticated tool could be devised by using the DWD Model as a long-term Planning Model to evaluate the sustainability of alternative options for meeting changes in demand for various agricultural and forest products. This could be achieved by balancing agricultural extensification and intensification, the

162 *Methodologies, Models and Instruments*

intensity of grazing, and wood harvesting in different layers of open forests. It could be run on a laptop computer or other PC without the need for sophisticated GIS capabilities.

A forest planning model

The governments of Senegal, Tanzania and Uganda, the three countries studied in this project, are currently devolving responsibility for managing forests from state institutions to local institutions, and they are typical of other governments in developing countries. However, most local communities currently lack the skills and resources needed to comply with these new obligations. The Planning Model outlined above could be adapted to identify those areas of open forest appropriate for long-term forest management and the potential yields obtainable from them.

Conclusions

This chapter has described a set of rational modelling techniques for evaluating the sustainability of villages in open forestlands in Sub-Saharan Africa. Despite data limitations, the need to integrate different types of spatial data, and the uncertainty associated with the activities of multiple users exploiting multiple layers of vegetation for multiple purposes, it is clear that the combined use of environmental and GIS models can make an important contribution in this field. Furthermore, it can provide the basis for practical planning techniques. The general methodology of GIS modelling employed here could also be applied in other settings after appropriate modification and development.

Three important qualifications should be mentioned. Firstly, the approach taken here has assumed that each village is largely self-sufficient in supplying its natural resource needs. In practice, however, most villages obtain some income from outside, e.g. from relatives working in cities or even abroad. Secondly, to be tractable, the models depend on the existence of effective local and state institutions to curb the exploitation of many individual people and prevent the 'tragedy of the commons'. Thirdly, by their very nature, rational models can only capture some of the factors and relationships that characterise actual land use management in developing countries in general and Africa in particular. Nevertheless, by providing a basic framework for analysis and a common starting point for community discussion, they should make an overall positive contribution to attempts to make the use of open forestlands more sustainable.

References

Adams, M.E., 1996. Savanna environments. In: Adams, W.M., Goudie, A.S. and Orme, A.R., (eds.), *The Physical Geography of Africa*, 196-210, Oxford University Press, Oxford.

Ahlqvist, O., 2000. Higher resolution put into perspective, *Geoinformatics*, **9**, 34-37.

Chisholm, A. and Dumsday, R., 1987. *Land Degradation. Problems and Policies*, Cambridge University Press, Cambridge.

Department of the Environment, 1987. *Handling Geographic Information. Report of the Committee of Enquiry Chaired by Lord Chorley*, HMSO, London.

Goodchild, M.F., Stayaert, L.T., Parks, B.O., Johnson, C., Maidment, D., Crane, M. and Glendinning, S., 1996. *GIS and Environmental Modelling: Progress and Research Issues*, GIS World Books, Fort Collins.

Grainger, A., 1992. Characterization and assessment of desertification processes. In: Chapman, G.P. (ed.), *Proceedings of Conference on Grasses of Arid and Semi-Arid Regions*, Linnean Society, London, 17-33, John Wiley, Chichester.

Grainger, A., 1993. *Controlling Tropical Deforestation*, Earthscan Publications, London.

Kidner, D.B. and Higgs, G. (eds.), 2001. *Proceedings of GIS Research UK 2001*, University of Glamorgan.

Lanly, J.P., 1982. *Tropical Forest Resources*, FAO Forestry Paper No. 30, FAO, Rome.

Openshaw, S. and Abrahart, R.J., 2000. *GeoComputation*, Taylor and Francis, London.

Sankhayan, P.L. and Hofstad, O., 2001. A village-level economic model of land clearing, grazing, and wood harvesting for sub-Saharan Africa: with a case study in southern Senegal, *Ecological Economics*, **38**, 423–440.

Chapter 14

Community Participation in Rural and Urban Development

Robert Dixon-Gough, Reinfried Mansberger and Mark Deakin

Introduction

Throughout the chapters of this book, a number of themes have emerged within the context of land management and development in rural and urban areas. These can be summarised as follows. Firstly, both rural and urban development is a very complex process in both developed and transitional countries. Furthermore, the existing interrelationships between the rural and urban areas need to be carefully monitored and assessed to prevent unnecessary conflicts in the peri-urban regions. For this to be achieved in a satisfactory manner there is an important need for the development and implementation of methodologies, models, and instruments to enable satisfactory decision-making in rural and urban regions. It is also essential that these methodologies, models, and instruments be continually reviewed in the light of changing needs and different circumstances and a legal framework (either regional, national, or transnational) to be developed and implemented for all aspects of land development.

In most forms of rural and urban development, there is a conflict of interests between centralised legislation (either national or based upon EU legislation, protocols or conventions) and decentralised, community empowerment that takes the form of community partnerships or forums. Similarly, there exists a clear conflict between commercial development and social needs, together with considerations relating to the environment and ecology, both in rural and urban areas. Most forms of development should take into consideration both the infrastructural projects together with the need for sustainable development and the incorporation of environmental improvements. One of the most important ways of achieving these important goals lies in education and the capacity building that is necessary for land administration and land management.

It is important to remember that application software is being increasingly used and applied to rural and urban development. One of the most important of these is based on a GIS platform, which is capable of presenting a range of possible solutions to planners and land managers. It is, however, important to remember that software *per se* can never replace a land management or planning expert, but simply be a tool that facilitates decision-making.

Community Participation in Rural and Urban Development 165

This relationship between these themes can be summarised through an examination of two significant areas of research into rural and urban land development; the interrelationship between rural and urban areas, and the increased emphasis upon community participation in all aspects of land management and regional planning.

Rural and urban development

The problems of land development in peri-urban areas, in particular those of urban expansion and the application of GIS to their management has been described by Dixon-Gough (1996). The application of methodologies, models, and instruments to the development of new urban areas is of fundamental importance and has been addressed through planning and land management instruments developed by countries such as the Netherlands to provide equitable solutions for sustainable urban expansion (De Wolff, 2001). In contrast, Muczyński *et al.* (2001) consider the development of land in rural areas of transitional countries. Both incorporate the underlying theme of sustainability and the need to develop environmentally-friendly approaches based upon community participation. One of the problems of peri-urban areas is the role of agriculture and how it is affected by creeping urbanisation. Źróbek and Źróbek (2002) discuss the role of small farms within peri-urban areas, both in terms of providing environmentally-friendly zones within urban areas that increase biodiversity and maintaining the livelihood of farmers who wish to coexist with urban dwellers.

The concept of biodiversity within city limits is often neglected in land management and land development strategies. Harrison and Davies (2002) cite the conflicting perspectives of brownfield development and urban nature conservation in London. The London Biodiversity Action Plan was launched in 2001 to enhance the survival of 15 conservation habitats in London. The development of this action plan was required by the GLA Act of 1999, which required the Mayor of London to develop a Biodiversity Strategy as an integral part of development policies.

One of the greatest threats to such sites in the UK has been the need to redevelop 'brownfield' sites, described as 'wasted assets' by the Urban Task Force (1999) and the Urban White Paper (DETR, 2000). This introduces significant conflict of interests. For example, it is estimated that 24,000 new homes each year are expected to be built in or around London each year (DETR, 1999). This will place pressure both on brownfield and greenfield sites on or around London and give rise to considerable debate between the need for homes and the competing rationality of environmentally sustainable development (Murdoch, 2000). Whether these developments are planned for London or around any other urban area, nature conservation policies must become mandatory under any spatial development strategy.

The pressure upon urban areas is immense. For example within Central and Eastern Europe, 67% of the population live in cities (Buckley and Mini, 2000). As a result of former socialist policies, excessive urbanisation combined with a sharp decline in industrial output and the closure of many traditional heavy industries has led to extensive levels of urban poverty. One of the problems of urban development in

166   *Methodologies, Models and Instruments*

these regions is how to alleviate poverty and unemployment rather than how to encourage environmentally sustainable policies.

Antrop (2000) defines urbanisation as a complex process that transforms rural or natural landscapes into urban and industrial ones, that have patterns controlled by the physical limitations of the sites and the transportation links. The modelling of this process has proved to be very complex, especially when taking into consideration the relationship between urban and rural areas and the growing awareness of spatial and environmental planning (SPESP, 2000; Pacione, 2001).

Whilst urban and peri-urban areas are under increasing threat of redevelopment and development, rural areas face equally serious changes. One such threat has been identified by Paquette and Domon (2003) in the form of changing ruralities and changing social compositions. As many rural areas are transformed from 'productivist to post-productivist' (Halfacree and Boyle, 1998) or from 'rural to post-rural (Murdoch and Pratt, 1993) there is increasing influence of urban and non-farming interests in rural areas. This is the direct result of in-migration of segments of the urban population to the countryside, from which has emerged social demands for new functions and services. These coincide yet conflict with the idyllic representations of the countryside that has proved such an attraction to the former urban dwellers (O'Rourke, 1999). Whilst landscape aesthetics attract rural in-migration, it had yet to be resolved to what extent this process will influence future landscape development or, indeed, whether the process will lead to a form of rural 'preservation'. This would inhibit any form of rural development that might detract from the perceived values of the rural idyll.

That the rural sector is in decline across Europe is generally accepted. Terluin and Post (2000) provide evidence of losses in population and jobs that are largely associated with the decline in employment in the agricultural sector. However, rural development policies in some areas have lead to a growing diversity of employment in the manufacturing and services sectors (Terluin, 2003). Although these opportunities did not fully compensate for the loss of jobs in the agricultural sector, many rural regions outperformed employment growth in urban areas. This growth is paralleled with other changes, some of which have been addressed above. Changing patterns of land ownership (in some cases, community ownership of woodland or grazing lands around villages), coupled with in-migration have resulted in a form of 'rural restructuring' (Bor *et al.*, 1997). The fundamental problem is whether that rural restructuring is part of a more general rural development process or a 'natural' evolutionary process of landscape change.

Decentralisation and community empowerment

In Chapter 2, Home introduced the concept of partnerships as a means of developing community participation in land development activities. Examples of such forms of community participation through the action of partnerships and forums were described at length by Dixon-Gough (2001). Although this discussion was primarily related to coastal zone management, the discussion emphasised the political dimensions of

Community Participation in Rural and Urban Development 167

community participation both within and across transnational boundaries. This theme is also the subject of discussion by Scott (2003) who considers the problems faced by agricultural communities. Many of Europe's rural communities are increasingly turning towards community-based local action and development solutions to face the challenges of the re-structuring of agriculture. This has led to a collective responsibility between people and the places where they live and work leading to a greater say in their economic and social well-being (Murray and Greer, 1997). There are interesting parallels here between the response of the rural communities and that of the urban communities in attempting to form community action groups to conserve 'wasteland habitats' (Urban Wildlife Partnership, 1999).

Partnerships have also become an accepted mechanism for the delivery of public policy in most western countries. Throughout the UK, partnerships have become embedded as policy vehicles for such diverse agendas as urban regeneration and social inclusion, and the implementation of rural development policies (Edwards *et al.*, 2001). The emergence of partnerships has been reflected in a growing shift throughout Europe from government to governance (Marsden and Murdoc, 1998; Murdoch and Abram, 1998). This is a recognition of the changing nature of 'consensus politics' and implications of economic, social and political changes, which have transformed the ways in which policies are made and delivered (Greer, 2001). With respect to methodologies, models and instruments for land development, community participation is an acknowledgement of the changing nature of public policy and administration. Furthermore, it emphasises the interrelationship between decisions taken at local, regional, and transnational levels, and is associated with an increased level of fragmentation in the delivery of policies (Hart and Murray, 2000).

Conclusion

Community participation can be viewed as a force for good providing it can be managed effectively and is not simply a forum for protest. When combined with other tools, such as the introduction of GIS to present alternatives, together with their environmental impact and likely effects upon all aspects relating to the community, community participation can be a real advantage in planning rural and urban development. Such a combination of community participation and software tools has been extensively used and applied in major projects such as land consolidation and urban readjustment. In such projects, the role of community participation can lead to significant environmental benefits, such as the restructuring of drainage networks to their former positions as flood alleviation schemes, or the introduction of green corridors within urban areas.

Finally, land management is invasive of all forms of rural and urban development, whether through models, methodologies, or the evolution of new or revised instruments. Land management effectively brings together land administration, with its dependence upon legal instruments and procedures and land development, which embraces the economics of land together with social and environmental considerations.

168 *Methodologies, Models and Instruments*

References

Antrop, M., 2000. Changing patterns in the urbanised countryside of Western Europe, *Landscape Ecology*, **15**, 257–270.

Bor, W., Bryden, J. and Fuller, A., 1997. *Rethinking Rural Human Resource Management: the Impact of Globalisation and Rural Restructuring on Rural Education and Training in Western Europe*, Mansholt Institute, Wageningen.

Buckley, R. and Mini, F., 2000. *From Commissars to Mayors: Cities in the Transition Economies*, Infrastructure Sector Unit, Europe and Central Asia Region, The World Bank, Washington, D.C.

Department of the Environment, Transport and the Regions, 1999. *Projection of Households in England 2021*, DETR, London.

Department of the Environment, Transport and the Regions, 2000. *Urban White Paper - Our Towns and Cities: the Future. Delivering an Urban Renaissance*, HMSO, London.

De Wolff, H., 2001. Development of land for new urban areas: in search of a new approach. In: Dixon-Gough, R.W. and Mansberger, R., (eds.), *Transactions in International Land Management*, **2**, 81-98.

Dixon-Gough, R.W., 1996. The role of spatial information management in assessing land use problems in the urban periphery. In: Tayama, T. and Weiss, E. (eds.), *Land Use Problems in the Urban Periphery*, 77-90, Peter Lang, Frankfurt am Main.

Dixon-Gough, R.W., 2001. Regional and international conflicts within the coastal zone. A case for partnerships and European-wide co-operation. In: Dixon-Gough, R.W., (ed.), *European Coastal Zone Management: Partnership Approaches*, Ashgate Publishing Ltd., Aldershot.

Edwards, B., Goodwin, M., Pemberton, S. and Woods, M., 2001. *Partnerships*, power and scale in rural governance, *Environment and Planning C*, **19**, 289-310.

Greer, J., 2001. Whither partnership governance in Northern Ireland? *Environment and Planning C*, **19**, 751-770.

Halfacree, K. and Boyle, P., 1998. Migration, rurality and the post-productivist countryside. In: Boyle, P. and Halfacree, K. (eds.), *Migration into Rural Areas: Theories and Issues*, 1-20, John Wiley, Chichester.

Harrison, C. and Davies, G., 2002. Conserving biodiversity that matters: Practitioners' perspectives on brownfield development and urban nature conservation in London, *Journal of Environmental Management*, **65**, 95-108.

Hart, M. and Murray, M., 2000. *Local Development in Northern Ireland - The Way Forward*, Northern Ireland Economic Council, Belfast.

Marsden, T. and Murdoch, J., 1998. Editorial: the shifting nature of rural governance and community participation, *Journal of Rural Studies*, **14**, 1-4.

Muczyński, A., Surowiec, S. and Zebrowski, W., 2001. Land management in rural areas of Poland: background to economic transformation in the nineties. In: Dixon-Gough, R.W. and Mansberger, R., (eds.), *Transactions in International Land Management*, **2**, 99-110.

Murdoch, J., 2000. Space against time: competing rationalities in planning for housing, *Transactions of the Institute of British Geographers*, **25**, 503-520.

Murdoch, J. and Abram, S., 1998. Defining the limits of community governance, *Journal of Rural Studies*, **14**, 41-50.

Murdoch, J. and Pratt, C., 1993. Rural studies, modernism, postmodernism and the 'post rural', *Journal of Rural Studies*, **9**, 411-427.

Murray, M. and Greer, J., 1997. Planning and community-led rural development in Northern Ireland, *Planning Practice and Research*, **12**, 393-400.

Community Participation in Rural and Urban Development   169

O'Rourke, E., 1999. Changing identities, changing landscapes: human-land relations in transition in the Aspre, Rousillon, *Ecumene*, **6**, 29-50.

Pacione, M., 2001. *Urban Geography: A Global Perspective*, Routledge, London.

Paquette, S. and Domon, G., 2003. Changing ruralities, changing landscapes: exploring social recomposition using a multi-scale approach, *Journal of Rural Studies*, **19**(4), 425-444.

Scott, M., 2003. Building institutional capacity in rural Northern Ireland: the role of partnership governance in the LEADER II programme, *Journal of Rural Studies,* Article in Press.

SPESP, 2000. *Study Programme on European Spatial Planning (SPESP)*, Final Report, 31 March 2000 (http://www.nordregio.a.se).

Terluin, I., 2003. Differences in economic development in rural regions of advanced countries: an overview and critical analysis of theories, *Journal of Rural Studies*, **19**, 327–344.

Terluin, I. and Post, J., (eds.), 2000. *Employment Dynamics in Rural Europe*, CABI International, Wallingford.

Urban Task Force, 1999. *Towards an Urban Renaissance*, Final report of the urban task force chaired by Lord Roberts of Riverside, E&FN Spon, London.

Urban Wildlife Partnership, 1999. *Biodiversity, Brownfield Sites, and Housing: Quality of Life Issues for People and Wildlife*, The Urban Wildlife Partnership, Newark.

Źróbek, R. and Źróbek, S., 2002. Management of agricultural real properties situated within town limits. In: Dixon-Gough, R.W. and Mansberger, R., (eds.), *Transactions in International Land Management*, Ashgate Publishing Ltd, Aldershot, **3**, 95-102.

Index

Action Plans 9, 106, 165
Africa 4, 146, 162
Agenda 21 5, 10, 123
Agribusiness 25
Agriculture 25, 36, 39, 40, 50, 142, 149, 159, 165, 167
Air Photography 20, 22

Bathurst Declaration 27
Biodiversity 10, 165
Biomass 99-101, 151-3, 155, 159
Boundaries 1, 3, 10, 22-3, 27, 31-2, 59-62, 64-72, 88, 108, 155, 157, 160-1, 167
Boundary Disputes 3, 59-73
Brownfield Sites 115, 165
Brundtland Report 121, 123, 125, 128-9, 132
Bulgaria 35-9, 45-6, 49

Cadastre 20-3, 25, 29, 44, 49, 53-4, 56, 58, 60-1
Canada 1, 16-17, 19
Central and Eastern European Countries (CEEC) 35, 49, 52, 57
Central Europe 2, 35-6, 39, 45-6
Change (Spatial) 139, 147-8, 154-5, 159
Change (Temporal) 137-45, 148, 154
Channel Tunnel Rail Link (CTRL) 104-20
Cities 5, 7, 17-18, 22, 31, 38-9, 77, 88-93, 104, 110, 115, 117, 121-8, 133, 139, 162, 165
Coastal Zone Management 5, 12
Collectives 18, 36
Collective Agriculture 36
Communities 2, 3-4, 10-13, 88-103, 106, 112-19
Community Participation 164-8
Community Strategy 104-20
Community Sustainability 146-63
Conservation 27, 109, 116, 122, 125-7, 152, 165

Co-operation 5, 20, 32, 37, 44, 46, 54, 77, 81, 85, 96
Co-operatives 13, 36
Countryside 92, 94, 97-9, 166
Czech Republic 35, 37, 49, 51, 52, 54

Deforestation 149-51, 153-4, 157-61
Developing Countries 16-23, 24, 31, 146, 149, 162
Development Plan 6, 10-11, 25, 75, 91, 105-6
Disasters 14, 27

Ecology 8, 24-5, 31-2, 97-101, 125-33, 149, 156, 164
Economy 8-11, 17, 23, 24-5, 28, 32-3, 36, 38, 49-50, 92-4, 96-101, 106, 108, 112, 116, 124-9, 131-3, 147-53, 167
Ecosystem 13-14, 128, 149
Education 1-2, 24-34, 164
Employment 89, 95, 114, 118, 125, 166
Environmental Capacity 121-2, 125-6, 129-33
Environmental Conservation 27
Environmental Impact Assessment (EIA) 126
Environmental Values 98-101
Estuary 5-15
Estuary Management 5-15
Expropriation 35, 57, 78, 79, 80-1

Farming 2, 18, 36-46, 50, 56, 65, 78, 86, 154, 156, 161, 165-6
Farms 18, 36
Floods 4, 5, 8, 10-12, 14, 139, 141-3, 167
Food Production 10-11, 25, 39, 146, 153, 156
Forests 4, 39, 40, 55, 57-8, 142, 146-63
Forums 6, 9-10, 13, 164, 166-7
Fragmentation 2-3, 35-48, 57, 65, 167
French Civil Code 51

Index

Geographic Information Systems (GIS) 4, 16, 25, 30-1, 71, 137-8, 142, 144, 146-63, 164-5, 167
German Civil Code 167
Germany 2, 35-48, 52, 57
Global Positioning Systems (GPS) 16, 22, 25, 30-1, 155-7
Greenbelt 88-9, 92-3

Heritage 108, 112, 114, 117, 121-3, 125-9, 132-3
Housing 17, 56, 76, 78-9, 94-5, 98, 100, 106-7, 112-14, 116-18

Infrastructure 2-3, 16, 18, 38, 60, 75, 81-2, 84-5, 91-3, 95-6, 98-100, 104-20, 125-6, 129-33, 137
Inheritance 3, 17, 56
Instruments 1-3, 25, 50-1, 57, 75-87, 96, 164-5, 167

Landowners 10, 12, 20, 45-6, 55, 57, 76, 78-80, 83, 112, 116, 119
Land Adjudication 18-20, 23
Land Administration 1, 17, 25-7, 49, 164, 167
Land Consolidation 2, 3, 25, 35, 39, 40-4, 46, 56, 59-74, 96, 167
Land Development 2-3, 25-6, 30, 75-87, 105, 164-7
Land Fragmentation 2, 35-48, 57
Land Information 21, 25-6
Land Law 17-18, 49, 52, 54, 56, 57
Land Management 1-2, 18, 22, 24-34, 85, 164-5, 167
Land Markets 2, 49-50, 97, 99-101
Land Ownership 1, 16, 35-7, 40, 45-6, 56, 78, 83, 166
Land Parcel 16-19, 22, 27, 36, 38-9, 42, 44-6
Land Reform 1-2, 16-23, 25, 30
Land Registration 17-20, 22-3, 43, 49, 54-8
Land Restitution 52, 57
Land Rights 2, 11, 16-18, 23, 26, 41, 43, 45, 51-2, 59-61, 66, 81, 162
Land Titles 16-20, 22-3, 36, 43-6, 52-8
Land Use Planning 4, 5, 11, 13, 147, 162
Landscape 38, 46, 92-3, 98-9, 128, 166
Law (Civil) 17-18, 41, 50-1
Law (Common) 17, 50

Law (Land) 17-18, 52, 54, 56
Legal Systems 49-58
Leisure 12, 89, 108, 115, 128-9, 148

Mediation 3, 27, 59-74, 119
Modelling 1-4, 8, 11, 36, 81-2, 88-103, 137-45, 146-8, 151-2, 154-6, 160-3, 166
Municipalities 3, 17, 75-85

National Planning Policy Guidance (NPPG) 91, 97
Natural Resources 25, 125, 146
Netherlands 2, 3, 39-40, 42-5, 51, 75-87, 165
Norway 3, 59-74

Partnership 1-2, 5-6, 12, 83, 106, 164, 166-7
Planning 1-2, 4, 5-15, 25, 27, 56, 59-61, 63, 67-8, 70-3, 90-1, 96-101, 105-7, 112-13, 115-18, 122, 124, 129-32, 147, 162-3, 164-7
Population 1, 25, 33, 39, 45, 51, 57, 89, 92-4, 98-9, 119, 142, 160-1, 165-6
Private Land Ownership 2-3, 6, 10, 16-18, 21, 35-6, 49, 52
Privatisation 17-18, 36, 45, 50, 57, 89, 126-7
Property 2, 11-12, 16-17, 19, 23, 26, 29, 36, 46, 49, 51-3, 55, 56-8, 60-1, 66, 80, 118, 128
Property Rights 11, 23, 51-2, 57, 128
Public Access 11-12, 60
Public Agency 6-7
Public Control 7, 16, 22, 32, 35, 62, 81-2, 126
Public Participation 4, 10, 12, 20, 44, 90, 105-6, 112-13, 117, 123, 133
Public Policy 5, 8, 27, 35, 44, 59, 78, 82-3, 92-3, 95-6, 98, 105-7, 114, 117, 167
Public Sector 5-6, 13

Redevelopment 4, 77, 104-20, 166
Regeneration 5-6, 8, 13, 94, 98, 107-8, 110, 113-14, 118-19, 155, 167
Rented Land 17, 21, 36, 41, 118
Retail 89, 94-6, 118
Rural Development 3, 56, 166-7

172 *Methodologies, Models and Instruments*

Settlements 3-4, 11, 46, 122-3, 125-8, 130, 132-3
Spatial Data 4, 21, 25, 148, 163
Spatial Development 75, 80, 107, 113, 165
Sustainability 4, 16, 25, 27, 114, 121, 128-32, 146-7, 151, 160, 162, 165
Sustainable Communities 3, 88-103
Sustainable Development 3-4, 10, 27, 31, 92, 121-36, 146, 164-5

Tenancy 38, 40-1, 45, 112

Thames Estuary Partnership 6, 9-11, 13
Training 1-2, 24-34, 55, 63, 68, 73, 117
Transportation 7-8, 10, 89, 91-6, 98-9, 106-8, 114-15, 117, 125, 129, 137, 166

Urban Development 1, 3-4, 6, 13, 18, 25, 27, 56, 75, 77-8, 80, 84-5, 121-36, 137-45, 164-7
Urban Infrastructure 2, 8
Urban Planning 6, 56, 137